Enjoy your

Zoe.

Feb 98.

BALLS,
BATS,
STUMPS
AND
STATS

BALLS, BATS, STUMPS AND STATS

AN OFF-BEAT COLLECTION OF CRICKETING ACCOMPLISHMENTS AND CURIOSITIES

Marc Dawson

an
ABC
BOOK

Published by ABC Books for the
AUSTRALIAN BROADCASTING CORPORATION
GPO Box 9994 Sydney NSW 2001

First published August 1997

National Library of Australia
Cataloguing-in-Publication entry

Dawson, Marc.

Balls, bats, stumps and stats: an off-beat collection of cricketing accomplishments and curiosities.

ISBN 0 7333 0597 0.

1. Cricket Miscellanea. 2. Cricket – Records. I. Title

796.358

Designed and typeset in 10/12pt Giovanni Book on Quark XPress by Anna Warren

Printed in Australia by Australian Print Group, Maryborough, Victoria

PRODUCED BY RICHARD SMART PUBLISHING, SYDNEY

3 2 1

CONTENTS

CONTENTS

AT THE CREASE

Batting at No.7 on his first-class debut for the South African province of Border in 1969-70, Ray Watson-Smith scored an undefeated 183 against Orange Free State at Bloemfontein. In his next innings, against Griqualand West, he again remained unbeaten, on 125. His aggregate of 308 runs in his first two innings without being dismissed remains a world record in first-class cricket.

Despite ten of its batsmen falling for a duck, Victorian side Koyuga managed a total of 74 against Stanhope in a club match in 1987-88. Paul McGann made 73 of the runs — the other came from a leg-bye.

Prior to the start of the 1985-86 series against New Zealand, Australian opener Andrew Hilditch vowed to remove the hook shot from his repertoire. He was out hooking for 0 and 12 in the first Test at Brisbane, and never played for Australia again.

Playing for Lancashire against Derbyshire in 1996, the New South Wales-born batsman Jason Gallian joined the triple-century brigade, registering the highest-ever score at the Old Trafford ground. His 312 beat the previous best at Manchester, set in 1964 by another NSW-born batsman — Bob Simpson, who made 311 in the fourth Test against England.

Despite Gallian's herculian performance, Derbyshire won the match by two wickets. The only other batsman to score more than Gallian against Derbyshire was Percy Perrin, with 343* for Essex in 1904, and he, too, finished up on the losing side.

During the first Test against the West Indies at Bombay in 1994-95, India's Vinod Kambli reached the milestone of 1000 Test runs in just 14 innings, two off the world record, shared by England's Herbert Sutcliffe and the West Indian Everton Weekes. Kambli's first eight innings in Test cricket were 16, 18*, 59, 224, 227, 125,

4 and 120. After ten Test innings, Kambli had accumulated a record 880 runs at an average of 97.78.

FEWEST INNINGS TO 1000 TEST RUNS

		M	100s	HS	Avge
12	Herbert Sutcliffe (E)	9	5	176	100.00
12	Everton Weekes (WI)	9	5	194	90.91
13	Don Bradman (A)	7	5	254	90.91
14	Neil Harvey (A)	10	6	178	111.11
14	Vinod Kambli (I)	12	4	227	83.33

MOST TEST RUNS AFTER TEN INNINGS

		M	100s	HS	Avge
880	Vinod Kambli (I)	9	4	227	97.78
878	Everton Weekes (WI)	7	5	194	87.80
833	Frank Worrell (WI)	7	3	261	104.13
831	Sunil Gavaskar (I)	5	4	220	118.71
813	Herbert Sutcliffe (E)	8	4	176	90.33

In a B-grade limited-overs match in New Zealand in 1982-83, Mangapai batsman David Gillingham was on 75* with one over to go. A century seemed out of the question, but amazingly he was able to crack it. He struck six sixes off Clyde Crackett to finish on 111*!

In 1981 New Zealand's Lance Cairns hit a blistering century, for English club Bishop Auckland, off 36 balls in 38 minutes. Playing against Danish team Glostrup, Cairns reached 150 off 52 balls and finished with 174, an innings that included 15 sixes and 16 fours. His explosive knock was similar to one a year-or-so earlier when he recorded the fastest century in New Zealand first-class cricket. Playing for Otago against Wellington in 1979-80, Cairns scored 100 off 45 balls in 52 minutes. Out for 110, he hit nine sixes and 11 fours.

After four matches in the 1995-96 World Series Cup, Australia's Michael Bevan had made 178 runs without losing his wicket. In his next one-day international series — the 1996 World Cup —

Bevan made just 20 runs in his first four outings, at an average of 6.67.

In 1990-91 Sachin Tendulkar, aged 17, scored 159 on his debut in the Duleep Trophy for West Zone v East Zone. His innings saw him become the first batsman to score centuries on debut in all of India's three major domestic competitions — the Ranji, Irani and Duleep trophies.

Ranji Trophy	100*	Bombay v Gujarat	Bombay	1988-89
Irani Trophy	103*	Rest of India v Delhi	Bombay	1989-90
Duleep Trophy	159	West Zone v East Zone	Guwahati	1990-91

Tasmania's Ricky Ponting came 'oh, so close' to scoring a century on his Test debut, falling just four runs short — his innings terminated by an umpire's finger. Playing against Sri Lanka, at Perth in 1995-96, Ponting became the first Australian batsman to be given out lbw in the nineties on his Test debut.

AUSTRALIAN BATSMEN DISMISSED IN THE NINETIES ON THEIR TEST DEBUT

Roy Minnett	90	1st Test v England	Sydney	1911-12
Arthur Richardson	98	1st Test v England	Sydney	1924-25
Arthur Chipperfield	99	1st Test v England	Nottingham	1934
Ian Redpath	97	2nd Test v South Africa	Melbourne	1963-64
Bruce Laird	92	1st Test v West Indies	Brisbane	1979-80
Ricky Ponting	96	1st Test v Sri Lanka	Perth	1995-96

As many as five batsmen hit hundreds on their first-class debuts in Britain in 1995, and all were Australians. Three did so during the Young Australia-Somerset match at Taunton — Martin Love (181), Adam Gilchrist (122) and Shaun Young (110). The other two were Andrew Symonds, for Gloucestershire (161* v Surrey at The Oval) and Michael Bevan, for Yorkshire (113* v Cambridge University at Cambridge).

Brian Lara's first three centuries in Test cricket were all in excess of 150 — 277 v Australia at Sydney in 1992-93, 167 v England at

Georgetown in 1993-94 and 375 v England at St John's in 1993-94. His next four centuries in Test cricket all came during the calendar year of 1995, one against New Zealand and three against England. Again, all were big scores, the lowest being 145 (147 at Wellington, 145 at Manchester, 152 at Nottingham and 179 at The Oval).

A $300 stamp issued by Guyana commemorating Brian Lara's Test-record 375 against England in 1993-94

When South Africa toured England in 1965 two of their future stars played against them at Bristol. In the South Africa-Gloucestershire match, two teenagers, on a season's trial with the county, both posted impressive half-centuries. Mike Procter, on his first-class debut, top-scored in Gloucester's only innings with 69, sharing a 116-run partnership with Barry Richards (59).

When David Boon made a duck against Pakistan at Hobart in 1995-96 it was the 16th time in his Test career that he'd suffered the dreaded score. It was a new Australian record, eclipsing Graham McKenzie's 15 noughts.

DAVID BOON'S 'DREAM TEAM'	
Gordon Greenidge	Ian Healy
Graham Gooch	Malcolm Marshall
Brian Lara	Richard Hadlee
Viv Richards	Wasim Akram
Allan Border (c)	Shane Warne
Steve Waugh	

In the mid-1800s, an Aborigine named Johnny Taylor was regarded as one of the top batsmen in the region of New South Wales that is now Canberra. A member of the Ginninderra Cricket Club since the age of 12, Taylor had a sensational game against Queanbeyan in 1869, top-scoring in both innings (36 & 81). He three times scored nine runs off one ball.

In consecutive matches against Tasmania in 1995-96, the Queensland pair of Matthew Hayden and Martin Love plundered over 700 runs before being dismissed. At Hobart, Hayden (152*) and Love (185*) shared a state-record second-wicket partnership of 368*, and in the return match at the 'Gabba put on 365 for the same wicket. Hayden scored his 21st cent ry, a career-best 234, while Love (186) missed by one run equalling his highest score in first-class cricket.

The previous summer, Love made 187, also against Tasmania, sharing with Stuart Law (143) a Queensland-record third-wicket partnership of 326 — the highest stand in first-class cricket in 1994-95.

After producing the first century of the 1996 World Cup — 101 against England at Ahmedabad — New Zealand opening bats-man Nathan Astle then scored 0, 1, 2, 6 and 1. During the same tournament, West Indies batsman Keith Arthurton had an even more frustrating time, scoring just two runs in five innings, for an average of 0.40. His scores were 1, 0, 0, 1 and 0.

When Michael Slater scored his maiden Test-match double-hun-dred, he etched his name in the history books by recording Australia's 500th Test century. His 219, against Sri Lanka at Perth in 1995-96, was also a record score in a Test at the WACA, beat-ing David Boon's 200 against New Zealand in 1989-90.

AUSTRALIA'S 500th TEST-MATCH CENTURY

1st	Charles Bannerman	165*	v England	Melbourne	1876-77
50th	Charles Macartney	137	v South Africa	Sydney	1910-11
100th	Bill Ponsford	183	v West Indies	Sydney	1930-31
200th	Neil Harvey	204	v West Indies	Kingston	1954-55
300th	Greg Chappell	247	v New Zealand	Wellington	1973-74
400th	Graeme Wood	172	v England	Nottingham	1985
500th	Michael Slater	219	v Sri Lanka	Perth	1995-96

Appearing as guest players for a Malaysian team in the inaugural 'Super Eights' tournament in Kuala Lumpur in 1996 were Allan Border and the Sri Lankan pair of Sanath Jayasuriya and Aravinda de Silva. All made ducks in the first match.

In the summer of 1932-33, England's Walter Hammond became the first batsman to score 1000 Test runs in one season. His tally of 1003 runs, at the extraordinary average of 111.44, was scored in two series — 440 runs from five Tests against Australia and 563 runs in two Tests against New Zealand.

Freddie Withall, a 64-year-old English club cricketer, scored his maiden century (107*) for the Alexandra Park 3rd XI against Old

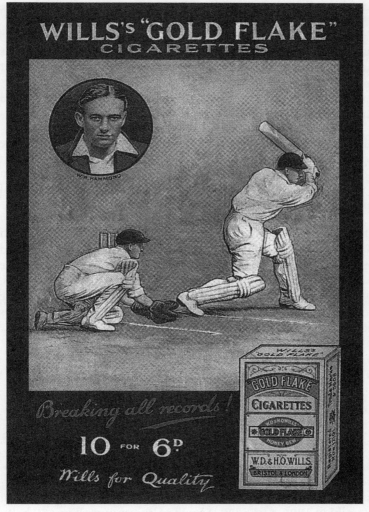

An early cigarette advertisement featuring England batsman Walter Hammond. During his first-class career, the England and Gloucestershire batsman shared in a 100-run partnership for all 10 wickets, contributing an individual century in each of them.

Stationers in 1987. Withall had been with the club since the late 1930s.

Australia's Herbie Collins appeared in 19 Test matches and was never dismissed for a duck. His 1352 runs is the highest number in a completed Test career that's free of the unwanted score. Another Australian, Jim Burke, played in 24 Tests and progressed through 44 innings at the highest level without a duck.

Six of South Africa's batsmen were dismissed for a duck in the second innings of the first Test against India at Ahmedabad in 1996-97. This equalled the Test record for the most ducks in an innings, established by Pakistan against the West Indies at Karachi in 1980-81.

During Sri Lanka's domestic summer of 1994-95, Romesh Kaluwitharana topped 1000 first-class runs, hitting a world record-equalling ten consecutive half-centuries. Keeping pace with 'Kalu' was Marvan Atapattu, who also made 1000 runs, stringing together seven successive first-class fifties. He made five centuries, topping the national first-class averages, with 1304 runs at 86.93.

MOST FIFTIES (10) IN CONSECUTIVE FIRST-CLASS INNINGS

Ernest Tyldesley	144, 69, 144*, 226, 51, 131, 131, 106, 126, 81	1926
Don Bradman	132, 127*, 201, 57*, 115, 107, 81, 146, 187, 98	1947-48/1948
Romesh Kaluwitharana	54*, 55, 52, 65, 71, 67, 72, 92*, 142, 70	1994-95

Batting for the first time in a match for Pakistan, teenage leg-spinner Shahid Afridi scored the fastest century in a one-day international, against Sri Lanka in the Four Nations Tournament at Nairobi in 1996. Afridi (102) reached his century off just 37 balls, taking from Sanath Jayasuriya the record he had set only months before, against Pakistan in Singapore. Although Afridi failed to break Jayasuriya's record for the fastest fifty, by one ball, he smashed the century-record by an incredible 11 deliveries. On

> **QUOTE**
> *"I didn't come here to slog. My main job is to be a spinner,*
> *but obviously I've found I can bat as well."*
>
> — Shahid Afridi

hand to witness the onslaught was Jayasuriya himself, who was belted for 43 runs off two overs. In all, Afridi faced 40 balls, with 12 deliveries not scored off. He equalled Jayasuriya's world-record of 11 sixes, and hit six fours, two twos and nine singles.

SHAHID AFRIDI'S HISTORY-MAKING INNINGS BALL-BY-BALL

• 6 1 • 4 • • 6 • • 6 6 1 1 6 6 2 6 4 4 • • 6 6 1 4 1 1 • 4 1 6 • 6 • 2 4 1 • W

FASTEST HUNDREDS IN ONE-DAY INTERNATIONALS

Balls				
37	Shahid Afridi	Pakistan v Sri Lanka	Nairobi	1996-97
48	Sanath Jayasuriya	Sri Lanka v Pakistan	Singapore	1995-96
62	Mohammad Azharuddin	India v New Zealand	Baroda	1988-89
67	Basit Ali	Pakistan v West Indies	Sharjah	1993-94
69	Javed Miandad	Pakistan v India	Lahore	1983-84

In the same year that Jayasuriya and Afridi established a new benchmark for the highest number of sixes in a one-day international, along came Wasim Akram who broke the long-standing record for most sixes in a Test innings. Playing against Zimbabwe at Sheikhupura in 1996-97, he hit 12 sixes in his unbeaten 257*, beating the 10 scored by Walter Hammond at Auckland in 1932-33. During his world-record innings, the Pakistan captain and Saqlain Mushtaq put on 313 for the eighth wicket, smashing the previous Test record of 246, by England's Les Ames (137) and 'Gubby' Allen (127) against New Zealand at Lord's in 1931. Wasim's score was the highest innings by a No.8 batsman in Test cricket and, at the time, he commanded the lowest career-batting average (19) for a batsman scoring a double-century. Saqlain's contribution in the record-breaking stand was just 79 — the highest partnership in a Test in which one of the contributors didn't score a hundred.

HIGHEST TEST SCORES FOR EACH BATTING POSITION

1	364	Len Hutton	England v Australia	The Oval	1938
2	325	Andy Sandham	England v West Indies	Kingston	1929-30
3	375	Brian Lara	West Indies v England	St John's	1993-94
4	307	Bob Cowper	Australia v England	Melbourne	1965-66
5	304	Don Bradman	Australia v England	Leeds	1934
6	250	Doug Walters	Australia v New Zealand	Christchurch	1976-77
7	270	Don Bradman	Australia v England	Melbourne	1936-37
8	257*	Wasim Akram	Pakistan v Zimbabwe	Sheikhupura	1996-97
9	173	Ian Smith	New Zealand v India	Auckland	1989-90
10	117	Walter Read	England v Australia	The Oval	1884
11	68*	Richard Collinge	New Zealand v Pakistan	Auckland	1972-73

MOST SIXES IN AN INNINGS

Test

12	Wasim Akram	257*	India v Zimbabwe	Sheikhupura	1996-97

First-Class

16	Andrew Symonds	254*	Gloucestershire v Glamorgan	Abergavenny	1995

One-Day International

11	Sanath Jayasuriya	134	Sri Lanka v Pakistan	Singapore	1995-96
	Shahid Afridi	102	Pakistan v Sri Lanka	Nairobi	1996-97

Minor

39	Kevin Hutchinson	311*	Trinity College v St Paul's College	Adelaide	1989-90

In 1874 the great W.G. Grace agreed to use a broomstick instead of a bat in a game against F. Townsend's XI at Cheltenham. Despite the handicap, Grace still managed to make the second-highest score (35) of the match.

During the English summer of 1996, Leicestershire opening batsman Vince Wells narrowly missed out on three double-hundreds in four innings. After scoring a maiden 200, against Yorkshire in the County Championship, he then became only the second bats-

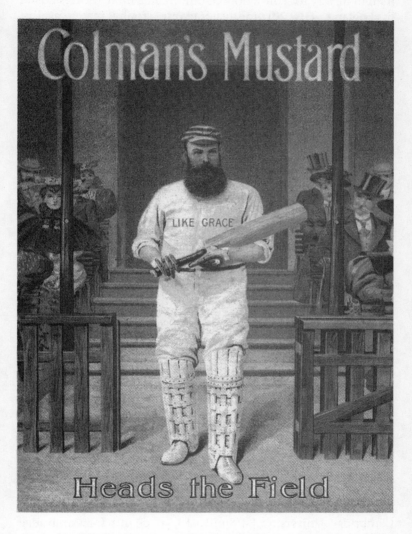

A mustard promotion from the 1890s featuring an image of W.G. Grace

man in history to score a double-century in a limited-overs match in England. His 201 in the NatWest Trophy match against Berkshire at Grace Road was just shy of Alvin Kallicharran's record-206 for Warwickshire against Oxfordshire in 1984. In his next outing, Wells continued his outstanding form, scoring 197 in the Championship match against Essex at Leicester. He later made 204 against Northamptonshire, his third double-hundred in six weeks.

DOUBLE-CENTURIES IN TOP-CLASS DOMESTIC LIMITED-OVERS CRICKET

222*	Graeme Pollock	Eastern Province v Border	East London	1974-75
206	Alvin Kallicharran	Warwickshire v Oxfordshire	Birmingham	1984
201	Vince Wells	Leicestershire v Berkshire	Leicester	1996

After scoring centuries in his first two first-class matches of the 1996-97 season, Victorian opener Matthew Elliott made his Australian Test debut, against the West Indies at Brisbane. He was out for a duck in his first innings — the 43rd Australian to suffer such a fate.

Michael Bevan also made a duck in the Brisbane Test, while another batsman named Michael Bevan was similarly dismissed, on the same day, batting for Sydney first-grade side Easts.

DEBUT DUCKS BY AUSTRALIAN OPENERS

Ken Meuleman	Only Test v New Zealand	Wellington	1945-46
Jack Moroney	1st Test v South Africa	Johannesburg	1949-50
Matthew Elliott	1st Test v West Indies	Brisbane	1996-97

Three teenagers scored centuries on their first-class debuts in England in 1996 — a record number in a single season. Steve Peters became, at the age of 17, the youngest player ever to hit a debut first-class hundred in Britain, with 110 for Essex v Cambridge University; Ed Smith, 18, made 101 for Cambridge against Glamorgan, while Northamptonshire's David Sales rewrote the record books with 210* v Worcestershire. He became the first batsman in the history of the County Championship to score a double-hundred on his first-class debut, beating Kent's Derek Aslett, who made 146* in his first match, against Hampshire at Bournemouth in 1981. At the age of 18, Sales became the youngest batsman to achieve a double-century in the competition.

DOUBLE-CENTURY ON FIRST-CLASS DEBUT

260	Amol Muzumdar	Bombay v Haryana	Faridabad	1993-94
240	Eric Marx	Transvaal v Griqualand West	Johannesburg	1920-21
232*	Sam Loxton	Victoria v Queensland	Melbourne	1946-47
230	Gundappa Viswanath	Mysore v Andhra	Vijayawada	1967-68
227	Tom Marsden	Sheffield & Leicester v Nottingham	Sheffield	1826
215*	Hubert Doggart	Cambridge University v Lancashire	Cambridge	1948
210*	David Sales	Northamptonshire v Worcestershire	Kidderminster	1996
209*	A. Pandey	Madhya Pradesh v Uttar Pradesh	Bhillai	1995-96
207	Norman Callaway	New South Wales v Queensland	Sydney	1914-15
202	Jeffrey Hallebone	Victoria v Tasmania	Melbourne	1951-52
200*	A. Maynard	Trinidad v MCC	Port-of-Spain	1934-35

Sales' extraordinary talent had previously been showcased, in 1991, when, as a 12-year-old schoolboy, he scored over 500 runs, with just one dismissal, in five consecutive innings — 63 retired, 102, 111 retired, 198* and 102 retired. In 1994 Sales scored a half-century on his debut for Northamptonshire's first-team in the Sunday League limited-overs competition. At 16 years 289 days, he became the youngest batsman to score a 50 in the tournament, an unbeaten 70 from 56 balls against Essex at Chelmsford.

S. Saleem created history in 1962-63 when he became the first cricketer to score a double- and a triple-century in the same match. The youngster performed the extraordinary feat in an inter-schools match in Hyderabad, with innings of 210 and 301.

All four openers were out for a duck in the first innings on the opening day of the County Championship match between Derbyshire and Northamptonshire at Derby in 1995. Former England batsman Kim Barnett went on to complete the first pair of his first-class career that began in 1979.

David Boon appeared in 107 Tests for Australia and scored at least one run in every match. Next on the list is Viv Richards who made a run in 98 consecutive Test matches.

In the Sheffield Shield match against New South Wales at Adelaide in 1970-71, South Australia's Ashley Woodcock and Ian Chappell were both run out for 95 in the first innings.

In a minor cricket match in Brisbane in 1961-62, Tim Nilsson hit an Australian-record nine sixes from successive balls, including eight from one eight-ball over. Playing for Northern Districts against Chermside, Nilsson scored 250, with 21 sixes.

Playing against Victoria at Hobart in 1996-97, Tasmania's Shaun Young was out for 113 — his eighth first-class century and the first time he had been dismissed after reaching three-figures in the Sheffield Shield. His previous six hundreds in the Shield had all been undefeated — 124* v South Australia at Hobart in 1993-94, 111* v New South Wales at Hobart and 152* v Victoria at Hobart in 1994-95, 100* v Victoria at Hobart and 175* v Queensland at Brisbane in 1995-96, and 108* v New South Wales at Hobart in 1996-97.

In 1921 Australia's Charles Macartney made 345 on the opening day of the tour match against Nottinghamshire. His collection of runs, in 235 minutes, remains an Australian first-class record for a day's cricket and was the world record until 1994 when Brian Lara (501*) made 390 runs in a day for Warwickshire v Durham at Birmingham.

Two years prior to Macartney's swashbuckling effort, a young

English batsman by the name of Greville Stevens scored in excess of 400 runs in a day at the University College School cricket ground at Neasden. Playing for Beta in the inter-college final against Lambda, Stevens remained unbeaten on 466, hitting 88 boundaries — believed to be a record number in any class of cricket. At one stage during his innings, Stevens clobbered 73 runs off three consecutive overs.

SCOREBOARD

Lambda v Beta
Neasden, 1919

BETA

R. P. Opie	c & b Page	0
E. M. Wingate	b Page	0
E. Edwin	b Moody	4
G. T. S. Stevens	not out	466
H. P. Slade	c & b Cave-Chinn	0
E. J. Masche	b Page	4
J. H. Kirkwood	st Tickner b Moody	6
C. S. Lazarus	st Tickner b Pegram	1
H. E. Hiscocks	b Page	0
A. Walker	b Cave-Chinn	23
C. G. Montgomery	b Page	0
	Extras	44
		548

In 1996-97 a 12-year old Indian schoolboy made 400 runs in a day in a junior tournament in Chennai. Deepak Choughale, an opening batsman, made 400* for Karnataka against Goa in the Sportstar under-13 competition. He struck 72 boundaries and two sixes off 322 balls in 316 minutes.

Bill Lawry and Keith Stackpole opened Australia's batting on 31 occasions with a highest stand of 95*, against India at Kanpur in 1969-70. The 1302 runs they scored in partnership is the highest in Test history for a pair of openers who failed to post a 100-run stand.

During the second Test against England in 1996, India's Saurav Ganguly scored 131, becoming only the third batsman in history to score a century on his debut at Lord's. His team-mate Rahul Dravid made 95 in the same innings, falling just short of what would have been the first instance of two batsmen from the same side scoring debut Test centuries. In the third Test at Nottingham, Ganguly scored another century (136), becoming the first Indian batsman to make hundreds in his first two Test innings. Curiously, the only other batsmen to have performed a similar feat were West Indians Lawrence Rowe and Alvin Kallicharran, who did so in the same series, against New Zealand in 1971-72.

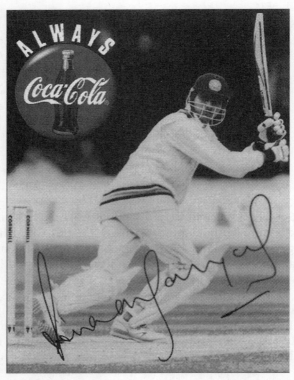

India's Saurav Ganguly during his innings of 131 against England
at Lord's in 1996

CENTURIES IN FIRST TWO TEST INNINGS

Lawrence Rowe (WI)

214	1st Test v New Zealand (1st inns)	Kingston	1971-72
100*	1st Test v New Zealand (2nd inns)	Kingston	1971-72

Alvin Kallicharran (WI)

100*	4th Test v New Zealand	Georgetown	1971-72
101	5th Test v New Zealand	Port-of-Spain	1971-72

Saurav Ganguly (I)

131	2nd Test v England	Lord's	1996
136	3rd Test v England	Nottingham	1996

CENTURIES BY DEBUTANT BATSMEN IN THE SAME TEST

Lala Amarnath (I) & Bryan Valentine (E)	India v England	Bombay	1933-34
Andy Ganteaume (WI) & Billy Griffith (E)	West Indies v England	Port-of-Spain	1947-48

Peter Taylor, who took eight wickets on his Test debut, against England in 1986-87, scored one of the fastest centuries on record in Sydney first-grade cricket. For Taylor, it was his maiden century — 101* in just 38 minutes for Northern Districts against Mosman in 1981-82.

In 1992-93 North Shore batsman David Horne hit a dazzling 255 off just 20 overs in a sixth-grade fixture in Auckland. His first hundred was reached off 33 balls and he managed a total of 24 fours and 21 sixes, including one from the first ball he faced. Two of his sixes hit cars, while four struck nearby houses.

Wollongong cricketer Paul Morgan scored a double-century for Balgownie's fourth-grade side against University in 1990-91, with all but one of his runs coming in boundaries. His 205 included 18 sixes, 24 fours and a solitary single.

In a Bolton League semi-final match in England in 1995, Kearsley batsman Steve Dublin hit 48 runs off one over bowled by Rob Slater of Heaton. Three no-balls that he received were dispatched over the fence for six, en route to the season's fastest League hundred, off just 35 balls.

Surrey batsman David Ward also collected 48 runs off an over during the summer, courtesy of Durham's Rob Jones in a friendly encounter at The Oval. Ward scored six sixes and two fours. Under playing regulations that governed the match, two no-balls, bowled by Jones, incurred an extra two-run penalty.

In the inaugural World Cup, in 1975, New Zealand skipper Glenn Turner scored 171* on his tournament debut, against East Africa at Birmingham. His opposite number, Harilal Shah, made a first-ball duck. Two matches later, Turner scored another unbeaten ton — 114* against India at Manchester, becoming the first and only captain to hit two centuries in the same tournament. Harilal Shah was the first captain to record two ducks in the World Cup — both first-ball, against New Zealand at Birmingham and in his next match, against India at Leeds. England's Mike Brearley also made successive noughts, in the 1979 Cup, and with Canada's Bryan Mauricette provide the only instance of opposing captains both making a duck in the same match (at Manchester).

Dominican-born Martin Jean-Jacques only scored one half-century in first-class cricket, achieving the feat on his debut. In 1986 at Sheffield, Jean-Jacques hit 73 against Yorkshire — the highest-ever score by a No.11 on his first-class debut — and shared a record 132-run stand for Derbyshire's 10th wicket with Alan Hill (172*), who also made his highest first-class score.

On the West Indies' third tour of England, in 1923, George Challenor became the first Caribbean tourist to top 1000 first-class in a season. His aggregate of 1556 runs, at 51.86, was double that of the next highest run-scorer on tour, Trinidad's Joe Small, who accumulated 776 runs.

Of the six hundreds scored by Challenor — three came in successive matches — his highest was against Surrey at The Oval where he carried his bat for 155*, sharing a 136-run last-wicket partnership with George Francis (41). Challenor remained unbeaten in the second innings as well, scoring 66* in an opening stand of 121 with Barbados team-mate Percy Tarilton, the West Indians winning the match by 10 wickets.

A decade earlier, Challenor (109) and Tarilton (157) had both scored centuries against the 1912-13 MCC tourists at Bridgetown, a match in which both teams recorded a 100-run stand for the last wicket — a highly unusual occurrence in any class of the game. In the Barbados innings of 447, Tarilton added exactly 100 runs for the 10th wicket with H.W. Ince (57), while the MCC's Arthur Somerset (55*) and 'Razor' Smith (126) matched the feat with 167 runs — the first-class record in the West Indies.

Opening batsman Wasim Jaffer made the record books in 1996-97 by scoring a triple-century in only his second first-class match. Playing for Mumbai (Bombay) against Saurashtra in the Ranji Trophy at Rajkot, the 18 year-old Jaffer hit 314, sharing a first-wicket stand of 459 with Sunil More (239). The previous record-holder was Victoria's Bill Ponsford, who made 429 in his third first-class match, against Tasmania in 1923-24.

When Tom Moody struck a pair of centuries (162 & 155) in the 1988-89 Sheffield Shield final against South Australia at Perth, his aggregate (317) represented a new Australian record for the most runs in a first-class match without a double-century. The record in all first-class cricket is held by Nottinghamshire's George Gunn, who made 354 runs (169 & 185*) against Surrey at Trent Bridge in 1919.

In the fourth Test at Adelaide in 1996-97, the West Indies' No.11 Patterson Thompson defied his record with the bat by hitting his first boundary — a six — in first-class cricket. Coming into the match with a career-average of 0.75 and a highest innings of 2*, Thompson went on to score an unbeaten 10. He even out-scored his team-mate Brian Lara (9), who was dismissed for his fifth successive single-figure score (2, 1, 2, 2, 9).

Despite having the services of Steve Waugh as his personal batting coach, Australia's Glenn McGrath had the unwelcome distinction in 1996 of becoming the first player to appear in 20 Tests without ever reaching double-figures in an innings. At the end of the one-off Test against India at New Delhi in '96-97, McGrath's batting record revealed a total of 38 runs, highest score: 9, average: 2.23.

McGrath finally broke through the barrier two Tests later, against the West Indies at the SCG. The No.11 almost tripled his previous best at Test level, scoring 24 — his highest innings to date in first-class cricket — and passing the milestone of 50 Test runs!

Glenn McGrath is a fine bowler, but his batting absolutely, utterly, unequivocally stinks. What's worse is that unlike Jim Higgs and Bhagwat Chandrasekhar, McGrath actually gives the distinct impression he is going to hit the ball. McGrath should be indicted for giving false hope to a nation. His second-ball duck against the West Indies in the first Test last week further cemented his status as the world's worst batsman.

— Michael Koslowski in the *Sydney Morning Herald*, on the day that Glenn McGrath went on to make his highest Test score

Glenn McGrath, we bow to you . . . but demand credit for your hidden batting success. After the *Herald* pointed out on Saturday that McGrath, statistically, was the worst batting pretender in the history of cricket, his Australian teammates did what any loyal bunch who spend a lot of time sweating for each other would do — they enlarged the article and stuck it on McGrath's locker in the dressing-room. The easily enraged McGrath then answered the knockers by smacking 24 of the most crowd-pleasing runs witnessed for many a season ... it took an old-fashioned humiliation by a ratbag column to give McGrath the runs, so to speak.

— Michael Koslowski, in the following edition of the *Sydney Morning Herald*

Playing for the Marin club in the United States in 1988, New South Wales batsman Wayne Seabrook scored 201*, one of the few double-centuries on record in the history of the Northern California Cricket Association.

South African batsman 'Dave' Nourse, who made his Test debut in 1902-03, had to wait a record 19 years before scoring his maiden century. In the second Test against Australia at Johannesburg in 1921-22, Nourse became the first South African left-hander to make a Test hundred (111), achieving the milestone in his 63rd innings.

Adelaide's Prince Alfred College can lay claim to being Australia's top breeding-ground for first-class cricketers with over 80 of its students making the grade, and four progressing to the position of Australian Test captain — Joe Darling, Clem Hill, Ian Chappell and Greg Chappell.

The annual fixture between Prince Alfred College (PAC) and St Peter's College, that began in 1867, is an institution in Adelaide, producing many fine individual and team performances:

• Joe Darling scored 252 for PAC against St Peter's in 1885-86 — at the time the highest individual score in South Australia. He added 278 runs for the second wicket with A.S.J. Fry (125), a record in Australia until 1890-91, while PAC's innings of 500 was then the highest total on record in the state.

• Clem Hill, aged 16, made 360* in 1893-94 — the world-record score in inter-schools cricket until 1904-05.

• After scoring a triple-century (311) in 1904, Charles Dolling made 106 and 27* and took 6 for 69 and 7 for 74 in 1905.

• Greg Chappell scored 107 and took 6 for 61 in 1965.

• Five former students appeared together in two matches in South Australia's Sheffield Shield side in 1972-73 — Ian, Greg and Trevor Chappell, Ashley Woodcock and John Causby.

• In 1988 Greg Blewett became the first batsman to score a century in three consecutive seasons in the PAC-St Peter's fixture. The future Australian Test batsman's scores were 130* in 1986, followed by 138 and 195*.

England's Graham Gooch is the only batsman to have been dismissed lbw on 50 occasions in Test matches. In 215 innings Gooch was out lbw exactly 50 times, accounting for 23.92 per cent of his dismissals. Next on the list is his former team-mate David Gower, who lost his wicket lbw 36 times. Gooch's final lbw-dismissal came in his last Test match, the fifth of the Ashes series, at Perth in 1994-95.

BATSMEN DISMISSED LBW THE MOST TIMES IN TEST CRICKET

Batsman	Country	No.	Inns Dismissed	% lbw
Graham Gooch	England	50	209	23.92
David Gower	England	36	186	19.35
Gordon Greenidge	West Indies	35	169	20.71
Javed Miandad	Pakistan	33	168	19.64
Mike Gatting	England	31	124	25.00

Better known as a fast bowler, Ed Giddins once made 92 for his school, Eastbourne College, but did so in the most dubious of circumstances! Indignant that his batting prowess was being ignored, Giddins, the No.11 batsman, locked the regular No.5 in the toilet, strode out to bat at the fall of the third wicket and made his 92, an innings that won the match.

THAT'S
ENTERTAINMENT

QUOTE

"When I was watching Fred Astaire I used to think, here was a chap who would have been a great batsman."
— Len Hutton

When a galaxy of past and present Test players gathered at the SCG for a one-day match in 1994-95, it was an actor with little cricketing experience who stole the limelight. Appearing for the World XI — a side that boasted Michael Holding, Andy Roberts and Joel Garner — Ernie Dingo, star of Channel 7's *The Great Outdoors*, took three top-order wickets for 56 runs.

In 1977 singers Phil Everly, from The Everly Brothers, and Elton John played in a charity cricket match for the Vic Lewis XI against Kew Green. Lewis, a former orchestra leader and one-time agent for The Beatles, made 53 in this match — the highest score of his career — in a partnership of 90 with Elton John.

A few weeks after their wedding in 1956, Arthur Miller and Marilyn Monroe travelled to England, where the world's most famous sex symbol starred with the cricket-loving actor Laurence Olivier in the film *The Prince and the Showgirl*. The author of the original stage play (*The Sleeping Prince*) was Terence Rattigan, another big cricket fan, and occasional player. While in England that year, Monroe was feted wherever she went, and amongst the many invitations she received was one to attend a cricket match.

Kim Hughes shares his birthday with rock guitarist Eddie Van Halen. The former Australian captain and guitarist were both born on 26 January 1954. Ian Chappell shares his birthday with international heart-throb Julio Iglesias (26 September 1943), while England batsman Jack Hobbs and Hungarian composer Zoltan Kodaly were both born on 16 December 1882.

Before Paul Smith made his first-class debut in 1982, the all-rounder was faced with the daunting choice of joining the Lord's ground staff, or joining a friend and becoming a roadie with the American rock group Van Halen. He decided on cricket, while his friend went on to become chief technician to Eddie Van Halen, and according to Smith "making £400,000 a year and living in the Hollywood Hills."

When aged 17, Tony Lewis, a violinist and future England Test captain, had to chose whether to go on the road with the Welsh National Youth Orchestra or make his debut for the Glamorgan cricket club: "Music or cricket? It was a cruel showdown. Cricket won."

Indian actor Saeed Jaffrey, who appeared in the hit films *Gandhi*, *The Man Who Would be King* and *My Beautiful Laundrette*, was Master of Ceremonies at the official opening of the 1996 World Cup in Calcutta. His presentation skills, however, left a lot to be desired — while welcoming the twelve participating teams, he introduced South Africa as the United Arab Emirates, UAE as Zimbabwe, and the Zimbabweans as South Africa.

Abraham Sofaer, an actor who enjoyed a long and successful career on both the London stage and in Hollywood, formed his own cricket team in 1929 — the Stage Cricket Club. Some fellow thespians who played in the team included Laurence Olivier, Jack Hawkins and Trevor Howard.

The cast and crew of the hit TV show *The Bill* appear in a yearly cricket fixture, the trophy for which is on display at Bosun House — 'The Sun Hill Police Station' — in London, where the series is filmed.

Simon Rouse and Colin Tarrant, from the British police drama *The Bill*, at a friendly cricket match in Sydney in 1995

A SELECTION OF POPULAR TELEVISION SHOWS
THAT INCLUDED REFERENCES TO CRICKET

★ The Bill ★ Heartbeat ★ One Foot in The Grave
★ Yes, Minister ★ Water Rats ★ Home and Away
★ The Avengers ★ The Final Cut ★ Mirror, Mirror
★ Candid Camera ★ Frontline ★ Hale And Pace
★ Men Behaving Badly ★ Blankety Blanks ★ Ellen

British jazz legend Ronnie Scott was a cricket fanatic who gleefully recalled one occasion when his band performed at Swansea and three young men requested their autographs. They were the 'Three Ws' — Everton Weekes, Frank Worrell and Clyde Walcott — who were in town playing in a match against Glamorgan.

31

In 1996 the Australian Opera staged three slightly unusual performances, with a cricketing flavour, on ABC Television. Written by John Doyle (aka 'Rampaging' Roy Slaven), from *Club Buggery*, the 'mini-operas' paid tribute to Test cricketers Shane Warne, Allan Border and David Boon.

Border's retirement from first-class cricket was commemorated with *Border — The Opera*, performed by Australian Opera members Christopher Josey and Christine Douglas.

'BORDER — THE OPERA' Act V Scene V

Allan Border: My darling Jane I have a confession.

Jane Border: Tell me.

AB: Well, I, er . . .

JB: Spit it out Allan, you're wasting my time.

AB: I want to stop playing. It's getting too hard. My bones are all broken. My eyes are too slow. My muscles are aching. It's breaking my heart. The young men are laughing. The crowds think I'm stupid. I want a life. I have to stop now to have a life.

JB: You stop and I'm gone. You must think of me. How could I live here with you under my feet ruining my life? I married a sportsman. A professional, that's what you are. Now get out and train. Don't break my balls.

AB: I want to stop playing.

JB: You stop and I'm gone.

AB: It's getting too hard.

JB: You must think of me.

AB: My bones are all broken.

JB: How could I live with you here?

AB: I want to stop.

JB: You must never stop.

AB: Think of me.

JB: Think of me.

Evelyn Pratt, the widow of actor, and cricket fan, Boris Karloff, was awarded honorary life membership of the Surrey county cricket club in 1985. Upon her death in 1993 she bequeathed an amount of £5000 to two English cricket charities.

British rock icon Eric Clapton is a big cricket fan, who ran his own celebrity cricket team in the 1980s. The XI had a very distinctive emblem — Clapton's initials with a crossed guitar and cricket bat.

QUOTE

"My ideal fantasy of England when I am away from home is going to Lord's or being by the river with a fly rod. Those are the things that sum up England for me more than anything."

— Eric Clapton

England fast bowler Neville Knox, who played in two Tests against South Africa in 1907, was once the understudy to the first-class cricketing-actor Basil Foster for the production of a play called *The Dollar Princess*.

Ralph Richardson, the distinguished British stage actor, fancied a game of cricket every now and then, captaining one match on board a cruise ship. The film star was the skipper of a game between passengers and crew, and at one point demanded a change of direction, accusing the ship captain of deliberately turning around the boat so the sun shone in his players' eyes!

In 1939 Richardson starred alongside the former England Test captain C. Aubrey Smith in the cinema classic *The Four Feathers*.

The Four Feathers: *Grand adventure from A.E.W. Mason story of tradition-bound Britisher who must prove he's not a coward by helping army comrades combat Sudan uprising. Smith is just wonderful as tale-spinning army veteran.*

— Leonard Maltin (*Movie and Video Guide*)

General Burroughs: Do you remember Wilmington?

General Faversham: Wilmington?

General Burroughs: Fine old service family. Father killed at Inkermann, grandfather blown up under Nelson, an uncle scalped by Indians — oh, splendid record, splendid.

General Faversham: What happened?

General Burroughs: Well the general ordered him to gallop through the front lines with a message. Paralysed with funk. Couldn't move. General sent his adjutant, killed before he'd gone fifty yards. Sent his ADC — head blown off. Then he went through with the message himself, lost his arm. Ruined his cricket.

— *The Four Feathers* (1939)

The pipe-smoking cricketer-turned-actor C. Aubrey Smith with Australian Test player Vic Richardson (second from right) at the Hollywood Cricket Club. Also pictured are Desmond Roberts (left) and Jamieson Thomas.

In 1996 pop singer Chris de Burgh forked out £6500 for a cricket bat at an Allan Lamb benefit auction hosted by Tim Rice and Rory Bremner. De Burgh then returned the gold-plated bat to the former England batsman to give to his son.

QUOTE

"My cricketing career is about as distinguished as Andrew Lloyd Webber's trousers, I'm afraid. Highest score, 18; most wickets in a match, 2. Feeble, isn't it? But, by Christ I love the game and that's what counts." —

Stephen Fry, star of the TV comedies *Black Adder* and *A Bit of Fry and Laurie*

STEPHEN FRY'S 'DREAM TEAM'

Gordon Greenidge
Graham Gooch
Viv Richards
Barry Richards
Garry Sobers (c)
Ian Botham
Mike Procter
Rod Marsh
Dennis Lillee
Michael Holding
Shane Warne

Danny Wilson, who made his debut for Essex in a one-day match against South Africa 'A' in 1996, is the son of Errol Brown, the lead singer of the British pop group Hot Chocolate.

Australian TV actor Mark Little, of *Neighbours* and *The Breakfast Club* fame, was Hampshire's '12th man' in a first-class match against the 1995 Young Australians at Southampton. Little's honorary duties at the ground were filmed as part of a program item for the BBC television show *Gower's Cricket Monthly*.

On Channel 9's long-running quiz show *Sale of the Century*, a cricket question stumped a champion in 1996 and was denied a shot at a new Audi car. He was asked to identify the former Australian Test cricketer who shares the same surname as the creator of *Tubular Bells*. He failed to make the Bert Oldfield-Mike Oldfield connection and, as a result, missed out on the grand prize.

Australian actor, Michael Craig

MICHAEL CRAIG'S 'DREAM TEAM'

Len Hutton
Gordon Greenidge
Don Bradman
Peter May
Garry Sobers (c)
Allan Border
Ian Botham
Godfrey Evans
Keith Miller
Fred Trueman
Shane Warne

Peter Pears, the noted English tenor, listed as his most memorable achievement in life, the time he once scored an unbeaten 81 for Sussex Schoolboys against Surrey at The Oval. His long-time associate in music, composer, conductor and pianist Benjamin Britten was also a great lover of the game.

Imran Khan and his wife Jemima joined actresses Greta Scacchi and Toni Collette at the 1996 London premiere of the Hollywood film version of Jane Austen's *Emma*. Proceeds from the night went towards the rebuilding of Imran's cancer hospital in Lahore.

The British comedy outfit Monty Python made many a reference to cricket in their classic BBC television series, with at least three specific sketches on the game — *Ritual Idioting at Lord's*, *Pasolini's 'The Third Test Match'* and *The Batsmen of the Kalahari*.

'RITUAL IDIOTING AT LORD'S'

Jim (John Cleese): Good afternoon and welcome to Lord's on the second day of the first Test. So far today we've had five hours batting from England and already they're nought for nought. Cowdrey is not out nought. Naughton is not in. Knott is in and is nought for not out. Naughton of Northants got a nasty knock on the nut in the nets last night but its nothing of note. Next in is Nat Newton of Notts. Not Nutting — Nutting's at nine, er, Nutting knocked neatie nighty knock knock ... anyway, England have played extremely well for nothing, not a sausage, in reply to Iceland's total of 722 for 2 declared, scored yesterday disappointingly fast in only 21 overs with lots of wild slogging and boundaries and all sorts of rubbishy things. But the main thing is that England have made an absolutely outstanding start so far, Peter?

Peter (Graham Chapman): Splendid. Just listen to those thighs. And now it's the North East's turn with the Samba ... Brian.

Brian (Eric Idle): Rather. I'm reminded of the story of 'Gubby' Allen in '32.

Jim: Oh, shut up or we'll close the bar. And now Bo Wildeburg is running up to bowl to Cowdrey, he runs up, he bowls to Cowdrey ... and no shot at all. Extremely well not played there.

Peter: Yes, beautifully not done anything about.

Brian: A superb shot of no kind whatsoever. I well remember 'Plum' Warner leaving a similar ball alone in 1732.

Jim: Oh, shut up, long nose ... and now its Bo Wildeburg running in again to Cowdrey, he runs in. He bowls to Cowdrey, and no shot at all. A superb display of inertia there. And that's the end of the over, and drinks. And now what's happening? I think Cowdrey's being taken off. Yes, Cowdrey is being carried off. Well I never. Now who's in next? ... it should be number three, Natt Newton of Notts ... get your hands off my thigh, West ... no I don't think it is ... I think it's, er, the sofa ... no it's the Chesterfield. The green Chesterfield is coming in at number three to take guard now.

Brian: I well remember a similar divan being brought on at Headingley in 9BC against the darkies.

Jim: Oh, shut up, elephant snout. And now the green Chesterfield has taken guard and Iceland are putting on their spin drier to bowl. The spin drier moves back to his mark, it runs to the wicket, bowls to the table. A little short, but it's coming in a bit there and it's hit him on the pad ... and the table is out. That is England nought for one.

'FILM REVIEW — *THE THIRD TEST MATCH* (DIRECTED BY PIER PAULO PASOLINI, 1972, OVAL FILMS LTD)'

Just as Peckinpah has revealed the bloodthirsty violence bubbling beneath the skin of Edwardian man so, in a different way, Pasolini, rips off the MCC tie to reveal the seething cauldron of sex that lies beneath the shirt. Once his Pandora's cricket box is opened we find flying out from the pavilions and changing rooms of the first-class counties a positive miasma of sexual yearning, culminating in the classic Brian Close shower scene, which recalls Hitchcock's use of Janet Leigh in a very similar shower (without, of course, the presence of Basil D'Oliveira).

'Sex and the Single Wicket Competition' could be the subtitle of this movie, for we get revealing glimpses of John Snow (a fine performance this on a desperately slow wicket) and we see quite a lot of the old Ken Barrington. Of course the bedroom scenes were bound to cause trouble, as they did during the making — Geoff Boycott walked out filming a torrid 'innings' when he was on a pair at Headingley, and there were complaints from Alan Knott's Auntie — but on the whole, as Denis Compton has observed, the balance between bed and bat is well maintained.

— *Monty Python's Flying Circus*

In 1995 a one-time member of the Australian rock band Ol' 55 helped form one of the game's oddest cricket teams — the LA Krickets. With the assistance of Ted Hayes, a prominent Los Angeles activist, singer-songwriter James Manzie introduced the game to the residents of 'Justiceville USA', a co-operative village for LA's homeless. Manzie, who has played extensively for the Southern California Cricket Association, became the team's coach, and within a couple of months the LA Krickets embarked on a six-match tour of England.

A club cricketer from England's Huddersfield Central League was banned for life in 1996 after disrupting his club's annual awards and entertainment night. After receiving the award for best bowler, Stuart Morley apparently took exception to the routine of a Lancashire comedian, Charlie Ash, jumping on stage and starting a fist-fight. Morley was brought before a disciplinary committee and banned from ever playing with the Cleckheaton club, or from appearing with any club in the league until the year 2000.

The soundtrack for the 1987 Australian movie *Burke and Wills* includes 'The Cricket Quadrille', an item by classical composer Peter Sculthorpe.

REX HARRISON — CRICKETER AND ACTOR

Rex certainly looked dapper and self-assured in his blazer and cricket flannels, with his hair carefully parted in the centre, but his elegance of dress and the flamboyant 'fright-tactics' which he employed for his left-handed bowling style failed to uplift his cricketing skill sufficiently to justify his position in the 1st XI. His father's face must have dropped when he read the analysis of his son's cricketing abilities in the College Magazine: *R.C. Harrison: The disappointment of the season. His bowling has possibilities but owing to his temperament he has only 'come off' once. His batting is weak and his fielding, though good at times, is often very poor.* But Rex did, at least, inherit his father's enthusiasm for the game and has remained a devoted follower all his life.

— Roy Moseley, *Rex Harrison: The First Biography*

Australian radio personality,
John Laws

JOHN LAWS'
'DREAM TEAM'

Mark Taylor (c)
Sunil Gavaskar
Don Bradman
Brian Lara
Garry Sobers
Steve Waugh
Keith Miller
Ian Healy
Shane Warne
Malcolm Marshall
Dennis Lillee

QUOTE

*"I have been a follower of the game since just after the
Second World War when I used to wag school to watch
Bradman belt the ball to the boundary like nobody
else in the world."*

— John Laws

The cover-piece for 'The Village Rondo', a piano composition by
Matthias Holst published in the early 1800s, featured a pictorial
scene of children playing cricket. This is believed to be the first
musical item with a visual cricketing link.

It was once reported in an Australian newspaper that the former
Australian Test all-rounder Keith Miller was the only man in the
country who could whistle all of Beethoven's *Fifth Symphony*!: "I
don't know why, but ever since I went to a concert as a small boy
and found I could remember almost every note when I got home,
music has been an important part of the way I live."

As an air force pilot during the Second World War, Miller
made an unscheduled detour when on a flying mission over

Germany. He left his group, Squadron 169, and flew up the Rhine to the city of Bonn: "That was where Beethoven was born, and being a bit of a ratbag, I guess, I was just curious to have a look."

After a year playing Jesus Christ in an Australian production of *Jesus Christ Superstar*, Darryl Lovegrove spent his hard-earned money on a trip to the Caribbean to see the 1995 Frank Worrell Test series. After witnessing Australia's first-Test victory, Lovegrove attended a net session with the players, where it's reported that he bowled some 'passable off-spin'.

A game of cricket was played on the ice of the Antarctic in 1994 by members of David Attenborough's film crew during the making of the documentary *Life in the Deep Freeze*.

J.C. Williamson, one of the most revered names in Australian theatre, was an enthusiastic follower of cricket who donated two trophies for a first-class match in 1900, between Australia and The Rest at the SCG. A very occasional player, he was dismissed for a duck in one match he played in, for the Gaiety Burlesque Company against the Permanent Artillery XI from the Victoria Barracks in 1888.

Singer, Kamahl

KAMAHL'S 'DREAM TEAM'

Sunil Gavaskar
Bill Ponsford
Don Bradman (c)
Viv Richards
Graeme Pollock
Garry Sobers
Keith Miller
Rod Marsh
Ray Lindwall
Dennis Lillee
Bill O'Reilly

41

Richard Keigwin, who played first-class cricket for Essex, Gloucestershire and Cambridge, was once a housemaster at Clifton College where one of his students was Trevor Howard.

Before Howard passed away in 1988, the actor made a request that his ashes be scattered over the Lord's cricket ground.

In 1972 Michael Meyer was asked by his old school, Wellington, to put together a motley eleven to play an Irish side called the Pembroke Cricket club "a lovely lot they were, mad Irishmen." He co-opted Trevor, Tom Courtenay and Tom Stoppard, who was a very good wicket-keeper, and "seven non-famous people to do the bowling and batting." During play a storm hung over the pitch, but didn't fall. By the time Michael Meyer's side went in it was night-dark. Trevor found himself at leg slip and was nearly beheaded by a ferocious hook then, when he went in to bat, it was impossible to see the bowling and he was run out for nought.

— Vivienne Knight, *Trevor Howard: A Gentleman and a Player*

Rolling Stones drummer Charlie Watts parted with nearly £5000 at a cricket memorabilia auction in London in 1995. His haul of goodies included Don Bradman's 1934 blazer, for which he paid a record £3600, Jim Laker's Test cap and a silver trophy awarded to Jack Hobbs.

QUOTE
"Mick and I go for long walks where we talk about cricket. It's one of the things the family does together."

— Mick Jagger's father

Harry Cadle, an MCC steward, became the subject of some notoriety in 1985 after ordering two members of The Rolling Stones to leave the Press Box at Lord's.

QUOTE
"Vulcan's got more hits than Elvis."

— Queensland batsman Jimmy Maher, after his guest appearance on *Gladiators* in 1996

Delta, who starred in the Channel 7 television series *Gladiators,* is the sister of the giant New South Wales fast bowler Phil Alley.

Greg Matthews, the former Australian Test all-rounder, put in an unsuccessful bid to host a national television show in 1996. Having failed the test some years earlier to join the cast of *Play School*, Matthews indicated an interest in replacing Tracey Grimshaw as presenter of Channel 9's *Animal Hospital*.

The appearance of pop star Michael Jackson in Sydney in 1996 created cricketing history, with the New South Wales cricket team forced to pack its bags and play elsewhere. With Jackson booked for two sell-out concerts at the Sydney Cricket Ground, NSW had to play its Sheffield Shield match with Queensland at the suburban Bankstown Oval — the first occasion that a Shield match in Sydney was not played at the SCG.

One of the 'hottest' singles of 1996 was one by a former Australian Test cricketer. In his role as Channel 9's resident Indian cricket expert Mahatma Cote, Greg Ritchie recorded what was billed as the world's first 'curry single'. The CD included the song *'Like a Tiger'*, and came complete with its own sachet of curry powder and recipe for 'Bombay Kari'!

Two big-selling singles from 1966 contained references to cricket. *'I'm a Boy'* by British rock group The Who includes the line: "I want to play cricket on the green . . . ride my bike across the river."

The other hit with a cricketing flavour was the No.1 novelty song *'Jake the Peg'* by Australia's Rolf Harris: "And, also I got popular when came the time for cricket . . . they used to hold my trousers up and use me for the wicket."

In 1975 two of England's favourite television stars appeared in a charity cricket match at Lord's. Representing the President of MCC XII was John Alderton, of *Upstairs Downstairs* fame, while *The Goodies'* Tim Brooke-Taylor played for the President of Lord's Taverners. Both bowled a few overs in the match with no success, while Alderton scored nine, bowled by Mike Procter, and Brooke-Taylor made an unbeaten two batting at No.11.

QUOTE

"I have always loved our national game since I was a small boy. Many's the happy hour I spent watching Derbyshire in the early fifties (I would have preferred to seen them in the early hundreds, but that was very rare)."

— Tim Brooke-Taylor

Mike Leander, a British songwriter who produced hit songs for artists such as Gary Glitter, Joe Cocker, Marianne Faithfull and Gene Pitney, was a member of the MCC. With cricket his greatest love after music, Leander once said he would have gladly traded all his talents as a musician to open the batting for England.

'Snowy' Baker, who played first-grade cricket for Sydney University, later found fame and fortune in Hollywood. A champion swimmer, diver, polo player and rugby footballer, Baker lost to Johnny Douglas, a future England Test captain, in the middleweight boxing final at the 1908 Olympic Games.

In California, Baker starred in a few silent films, and passed on his horse-riding and whipping skills to leading actors such as Liz Taylor, Rudolph Valentino, Spencer Tracey and Douglas Fairbanks.

During a national tour in support of Melbourne singer Paul Kelly in 1996, The Blackeyed Susans temporarily lost their instruments. They eventually retrieved the gear — it was found with the visiting Sri Lankan cricket team!

SOME STARS OF STAGE AND SCREEN HAVE THEIR SAY ON THE SUMMER GAME

"There is, of course, a world of difference between cricket and the movie business. But I can assure you that movies entail just as much hard graft. The highlights are tremendous for both. I suppose doing a love scene with Raquel Welch roughly corresponds to scoring a century before lunch."

— Oliver Reed

"My first exposure to English summer madness came in 1968 when I was over here for the first time to make Where Eagles Dare. *Clint Eastwood expressed surprise that any game could be played for five days and then be declared a draw, so arrangements were made for interested members of the cast to spend a day at the Lord's Test. It was a mammoth non-event as far as I was concerned but I do remember thinking how sexy the players looked in their virginal white outfits."*

— British actress Ingrid Pitt

"I know absolutely nothing about cricket."

— Clive James

"My cricketing days are over now and all that is left are my memories. When other old amateurs talk nostalgically over pints of beer about the runs they've scored, the catches they've made and the wickets they've taken, I just sit and rub certain parts of my anatomy and open a fresh bottle of embrocation."

— Harry Secombe

"When in the middle of a good innings my batting partner hit an early catch towards me, the desire for laughs overcame all other instincts. I dropped my bat and caught the ball. Such a bold defiance of the sport had its desired effect on the umpire. He ordered me off the field. Later, I was called to his room for six of the best."

— John Le Mesurier, star of the TV comedy *Dad's Army*

"The only time I played cricket was at school when I was forced to, otherwise it was the whip."

— Jimmy Edwards

"I once captained a concert artistes' cricket team, consisting of myself, seven baritones, two tenors, and a child impersonator in plimsolls."

— Dennis Castle

"At the completion of our self-titled album we celebrated with a game of cricket. The studio became our oval. A piece of 4x2 wood became the bat, we rolled up some gaffer tape to use as a ball, and a guitar case was the wicket."

— Noiseworks drummer Kevin Nichol

"I love cricket as much as I love music. And through my love of music I've managed to make a much more successful career than I ever might have on a cricket field."

— 'Molly' Meldrum

WIDE WORLD
OF SPORTS

Bernard Bosanquet, who played Test cricket for England in the early 1900s, represented Oxford University at both hammer throwing and billiards. It seems, however, he had no time for golf or tennis, venting his spleen at both sports in a letter to *The Times* newspaper in 1914.

> The sooner it is realised that golf is merely a pleasant recreation and inducement to indolent people to take exercise, the better.
>
> Golf has none of the essentials of a great game. It destroys rather than builds up character and tends to selfishness and ill-temper. It calls for none of the qualities of a great game such as pluck, endurance, physical fitness and agility, unselfishness and esprit de corps.
>
> The present tendency is undoubtedly towards the more effeminate and less exacting pastimes but the day that sees the youth of England given up to lawn tennis and golf . . . will be a sad omen for the future of the race.

Ray Lindwall and Keith Miller — one of Australia's greatest fast-bowling partnerships — were both very fine footballers. Lindwall played rugby league for St George in Sydney, while Miller appeared in 50 games for the St Kilda VFL club.

In his final year at school in Sydney, Lindwall was the Marist Brothers athletics champion, winning both the long and high jump. He also captained the college's first-grade cricket and rugby league teams, posting 230 of the 571 points scored during the 1939 season. For St George, Lindwall scored seven tries and booted 123 goals in 31 appearances. In the 1942 grand final, the fast bowler played alongside his brother, Jack, who scored the Saints' only try in their 11-9 loss to Canterbury.

Bobby Chapman and Jamie Hart, who opened the bowling for Nottinghamshire in a Sunday League match against Somerset in 1995, are the sons of two Nottingham Forest footballers — Sammy Chapman and Paul Hart.

Teddy Wynyard, a noted figure skater, played Test cricket for England three times and appeared for Old Carthusians in the FA Cup final of 1881.

'Buster' Farrer, who played in six Test matches for South Africa in the 1960s, played tennis at Wimbledon. After scoring a half-century on his first-class debut for Border in 1954-55, Farrer gave up cricket for four years rising to No.7 in South Africa's tennis rankings. He made his Test debut, against New Zealand, in 1961-62.

Former England Test cricketer Mike Denness was a promising rugby union player, who appeared alongside a future international in his schoolboy side. 1974 was a big year for both players — Ian McLauchlan became Scotland's soccer captain, while Denness was made captain of the England cricket side.

Graeme Hughes played first-class cricket for New South Wales between 1975-76 and '78-79, and also represented his state at rugby league — one of only five sportsmen to have achieved such a feat; the others being Bill Ives, Rex Norman, Dudley Seddon and Lyall Wall. Hughes and his brothers, Mark and Garry, all played first-grade football for Canterbury-Bankstown and first-grade cricket for Petersham.

In 1973 Kepler Wessels was rated the No.1 under-16 tennis player in South Africa. Coached, at one stage, during his formative years by Hansie Cronje's mother, Wessels defeated a future tennis star — Johan Kriek — on his way to becoming junior champion.

Playing on the senior circuit in 1974, Wessels ended his tennis career during the Griqualand West Open with a performance John McEnroe would have been proud of. Trailing by two sets to one in a match against Cyril Rudman, Wessels stormed off the court in a rage to the sanctuary of his dressing-room. When he returned court-side he produced his racket with all the strings slashed. Wessels had used a pair of scissors to destroy the racket, and, ultimately, his career.

Former South African all-rounder Mike Procter played competitive hockey and tennis at school. His mother was a provincial tennis player, while his wife, Maryna, represented South Africa in the Federation Cup, rising to No.2 in the official national rankings.

At the age of 12, Viv Richard's son, Mali, simultaneously gained selection in Antigua's under-14 cricket side and under-15 tennis squad. He chose to go to Dominica with the tennis team.

Leah Martindale, the grand-daughter of former West Indies Test cricketer 'Manny' Martindale, came close to a world swimming record in 1995 at the National Championships in Bridgetown. Leah recorded the second-fastest 50 metres freestyle of the year, completing the swim in 24.97 seconds.

Warwick Armstrong, one of Test cricket's most successful captains, played VFL football for South Melbourne, appearing in the grand final against Fitzroy in 1899.

In 1996 the Australian Football League began its centenary season with a match at the MCG that paid tribute to a former first-class cricketer. The annual Wills-Harrison Trophy match, between Geelong and Melbourne, was named after Thomas Wentworth Wills and his brother-in-law and cousin, Henry Harrison, who in 1858 drafted the first rules of Australian football. Wills helped form the Melbourne club, and both he and Harrison played for Geelong.

At the same time he was captain of the Victorian cricket team, Wills umpired the first recorded game of Aussie Rules, in 1858, at Richmond Paddock. Wills also played first-class cricket for Kent, the MCC and Cambridge University.

Jonty Rhodes was a part of South Africa's hockey training squad for the 1996 Olympic Games. Before turning to full-time cricket, Rhodes was a member of South Africa's hockey squad in the early 1990s, and scored a spectacular goal that earned Natal the South African provincial title in 1991.

Australian Wallaby Matthew Burke, who made his rugby Test debut in 1993, played cricket at St Joseph's College, taking the new ball for the 1st XI.

While at school in South Africa, England Test batsman Robin Smith excelled at both cricket and union, forming a strong centre partnership with Hugh Reece-Edwards, who went on to win three rugby Springbok caps.

George Coulthard, who both played and umpired Test-match cricket, was a major figure in Aussie Rules football. Regarded as 'the grandest player of his day', Coulthard appeared for the Carlton club from 1876 in the VFA competition.

The famous cricket ground used by the Hollywood Cricket Club in Los Angeles was bulldozed to make way for the 1984 Olympic Games' equestrian centre.

It's been reported that javelin thrower Janis Lusis — who won gold for the Soviet Union at the 1968 Olympic Games — once threw a cricket ball approximately 150 yards. If it was ever officially verified, his throw would constitute a world record. According to *Wisden*, the 'unofficial' record is 140 yards 2 feet, by Robert Percival, in Durham in the 1880s.

Bobby Etheridge played in over 300 matches for the Bristol City soccer club and represented Gloucestershire at both lawn bowls and first-class cricket (1955/1956).

Sir Dallas Brooks, Victoria's Governor from 1949 to 1963, played first-class cricket for Hampshire, captained the Royal Navy at golf and was an Olympic hockey player.

Sir E.F. Herring, Lieutenant Governor of Victoria between 1945 and 1972, appeared in two first-class matches for Oxford University in 1913, and also played doubles tennis at Wimbledon.

The late motor racing champion Ayrton Senna had a long-standing association with a cricket club in England. Senna, who knew little about the game, used to frequent the Esher cricket club ground in Surrey where he flew his model aeroplanes.

George Lyon, eight times his country's amateur golf champion, scored a Canadian-record 238 for the Rosedale cricket club against Peterborough in 1894.

Cecil Payne, who scored a century on his first-class debut, for the MCC at Lord's in 1905, became Canada's amateur billiards champion in 1927, and the following year, amateur golf champion of British Colombia.

Asif Karim, a Davis Cup tennis player, represented Kenya in the 1996 World Cup.

In 1996 a grandson of Vinoo Mankad, the former Indian Test captain, played in the Indian Open Mens Tennis Championship and appeared in Sydney at the inaugural Australia Television Cup. Harsh Mankad comes from a long line of sporting achievers — his father, Ashok, appeared in 22 Test matches, while his mother, Nirupama, played tennis at Wimbledon.

Aub Carrigan, who shared a record second-wicket partnership of 430 with Ken 'Slasher' Mackay in a first-grade match in Brisbane in 1945-46, represented Queensland at cricket, lawn bowls and

Aussie Rules football. Of the four centuries he scored in first-class cricket, two were against international sides — 100 v England in 1950-51 and 169 v the West Indians in 1951-52.

William Evans made his first-class debut for Queensland in 1898-99 and a few months later appeared in two rugby Test matches against England. His brother, Llewellyn, also played international rugby for Australia and was once 12th man in a match for Queensland.

Ernie Hutcheon represented Australia in athletics at the 1908 Olympic Games and later played first-class cricket for Queensland, making his debut in 1919-20. George Hillyard was another first-class cricketer to appear at the London Games, representing England at tennis, while Essex batsman Johnny Douglas won the middleweight boxing final.

Adam Gilchrist once represented NSW High Schools at an Australian athletics carnival. The wicket-keeper was also a handy soccer player, captaining an Australian secondary school team on a tour of England and the United States — he later appeared for the Wollongong Wolves in the National Soccer League.

Queensland fast bowler Andy Bichel played both cricket and rugby league in the early 1990s. For several seasons he was a five-eighth and halfback for the Gatton club in Toowoomba's A-grade competition and once received a contract to play league in England.

Lindsay Hassett, who captained Australia with great success in the 1950s, played amateur Aussie Rules football for Victoria, and was the state's schoolboy tennis champion in 1931-32. Hassett's brother, Harry, also excelled at tennis, making the Australian Davis Cup squad.

A few months after taking five wickets on his first-class cricket debut for Hampshire in 1996, Liam Botham signed a three-year contract with the first-division rugby union side West Hartlepool.

Botham celebrated the New Year and his new professional sporting discipline by scoring a try in only his second match in Division One, in West's 24-8 victory over Orrell.

QUOTE

"I have enjoyed both cricket and rugby since my school days and perhaps everyone assumed I'd concentrate on cricket. It wasn't an easy decision to make and I'll always remember my first-class debut and the five-wicket haul against Middlesex, but I've always had a slight preference for rugby."

— Liam Botham

THE BOWLERS

On his return to Test cricket, at Harare in 1992-93, Zimbabwe's John Traicos picked up 5 for 86, including the wicket of India's star batsman Sachin Tendulkar — caught and bowled for a duck. For the 45-year-old spinner, this was his first Test match for 22 years and 222 days since playing for South Africa in their last Test before expulsion from the international scene. Tendulkar had not even been born when Traicos had taken his previous Test wicket — Australia's Laurie Mayne, at Johannesburg in 1969-70.

In the lead-up to the World Series finals in 1995-96, Glenn McGrath copped a hiding at the hands of Sri Lanka, conceding eight runs an over in the match at the MCG. He set a new Australian record for the most expensive bowling stint in a one-day international — 1 for 76, and he didn't even complete his allotted ten overs. The previous record-holder was McGrath's opening partner Craig McDermott, who twice conceded over 70 runs in one-day internationals.

WORST FIGURES BY AUSTRALIAN BOWLERS IN ONE-DAY INTERNATIONALS

9.4-0-76-1	Glenn McGrath	v Sri Lanka	Melbourne	1995-96
10-0-75-0	Craig McDermott	v India	Jaipur	1986-87
11-1-72-0	David Colley	v England	Lord's	1972
12-0-72-1	Ashley Mallett	v Sri Lanka	The Oval	1975
12-1-71-0	Max Walker	v West Indies	Lord's	1975
8-1-70-0	Adam Dale	v South Africa	Bloemfontein	1996-97
10-1-70-2	Craig McDermott	v New Zealand	Adelaide	1985-86
11-1-70-1	Paul Reiffel	v England	Birmingham	1993
11-0-70-0	Steve Waugh	v England	Lord's	1989

South Africa's Shaun Pollock began his role as Warwickshire's professional in 1996 by taking a record four wickets in four balls on his debut. Playing against Leicestershire in the Benson &

> ## QUOTE
> *"If someone had said I would make a start like that, I would have laughed at them."*
>
> — Shaun Pollock

Hedges Cup at Edgbaston, Pollock grabbed a match-winning 6 for 21, including four wickets in a row, completing a feat never recorded before in the competition's 24-year history.

New South Wales fast bowler Roy Minnett captured his best-ever figures in first-class cricket in his final match. Playing against Victoria at Melbourne in 1914-15, Minnett took 8 for 50 in the first innings and finished the match, and his career, with 10 for 84.

Anil Bhattacharjee, a medium-fast bowler who claimed the remarkable figures of 10 for 11 in an Indian first-class match in 1974-75, is a deaf-mute.

During the course of two Test matches being played concurrently in 1996-97, two debutant fast bowlers took record-breaking hauls of seven wickets in an innings. South Africa's Lance Klusener sent India to a crushing 329-run defeat in the second Test at Calcutta, with 8 for 64 — the fourth-best performance by a bowler on his Test debut and the best-ever by a South African. His record performance followed a horror stint in the first innings, in which he was belted for 0 for 75 off 14 overs.

On the same day, in Rawalpindi, Pakistan paceman Mohammad Zahid destroyed New Zealand in the second Test, taking 7 for 66 — the best debut-innings performance by a Pakistani. With 4 for 64 in the first innings, he became the first for his country to capture 10 wickets on his Test debut and, in what was only his fifth first-class match, made Test history by taking a world-record eight wickets lbw.

Michael Kasprowicz — who in 1992-93, became, at the age of 21, the youngest Australian bowler to take 50 wickets in a season — claimed a record 64 wickets for Queensland in 1995-96. His haul was the best by any bowler in state cricket, beating the previous record of 63 wickets set by Charlie Turner, for New South Wales in 1887-88, and equalled by South Australia's Clarrie Grimmett in 1939-40.

60 FIRST-CLASS WICKETS IN A SEASON FOR ONE STATE

Wkts	M	Bowler	State	Season
64	11	Michael Kasprowicz	Queensland	1995-96
63	7	Charlie Turner	NSW	1887-88
63	8	Clarrie Grimmett	SA	1939-40
60	6	'Chuck' Fleetwood-Smith	Victoria	1934-35

Charlie 'The Terror' Turner, and the grip that brought him a record 63 wickets for New South Wales in 1887-88. In all first-class matches that summer, Turner collected 106 wickets, average 13.59, and remains the only bowler to take 100 wickets in an Australian season.

In the Bicentennial Youth World Cup, played in Australia in 1987-88, New South Wales fast bowler Wayne Holdsworth topped the bowling averages with 19 wickets at 12.52. On consecutive days the young speedster claimed hauls of 4 for 36 (v New Zealand at Wentworth and v Pakistan at Mildura). Holdsworth tied with Pakistan's Mushtaq Ahmed as the tournament's leading wicket-taker.

Sri Lanka's Roger Wijesuriya bowled 586 balls in Test-match cricket, from which he gained only one wicket — Pakistan's Abdul Qadir, at Karachi in 1985-86. His average of 294.00 is the highest in Test history.

At The Oval in 1890, England's bowling attack for the second Test against Australia was opened by George Lohmann and debutant Frederick 'Nutty' Martin, both of whom would finish their Test careers with a bowling average of around 10.00. After taking 12 wickets on his Test debut, Martin made just one more appearance — against South Africa at Cape Town in 1891-92, where he bowled unchanged with J.J. Ferris in the second innings.

LOWEST BOWLING AVERAGES IN TEST CRICKET (Qual: 10 wickets)

		M	W	10wm	5wi	BB
8.73	'Father' Marriott (E)	1	11	1	2	6-59
10.07	'Nutty' Martin (E)	2	14	1	2	6-50
10.76	George Lohmann (E)	18	112	5	9	9-28
12.60	Laurie Nash (A)	2	10	0	0	4-18
12.70	J.J. Ferris (A & E)	9	61	1	6	7-37
13.00	Tom Horan (A)	15	11	0	1	6-40
13.91	Harry Dean (E)	3	11	0	0	4-19
15.00	Albert Trott (A & E)	5	26	0	2	8-43

Maties' bowler Stuart Hockley was denied the opportunity to achieve a hat-trick in a match in the South African Boland Premiership in 1995-96, when the next batsman — Kraaifontein's Terence Lazard — was too slow to get to the wicket, and was, therefore, dismissed 'timed out'.

In his first international match for Australia, fast bowler Jason Gillespie snared the prized wickets of two former Test captains.

Appearing in the Victorian Cricket Association's centenary Australia-World XI one-day match at the MCG in 1995-96, Gillespie clean-bowled Richie Richardson with the fifth ball of his first over, and later claimed Martin Crowe's wicket to finish with the impressive debut figures of 8-1-23-2.

In his 30-match first-class career, Queensland's William Evans only ever took eight wickets. But seven of them came on his first-class debut — against South Australia at Brisbane in 1898-99. The eighth bowler used in the innings, Evans claimed 7 for 70.

In a fourth-grade club match in England in 1984, two players with a combined age of 121 — Reg Hayter (70) and John Ball (51) — bowled unchanged to dismiss their opponents for 32.

Appearing for the East Torrens club in 1984-85, former South Australian cricketer Bob Blewett returned the miserly figures of 32-27-9-4 against Adelaide. Bowling in tandem with Neil Plummer, whose final analysis was 29-19-24-1, only 33 runs came off the bat in 61 overs.

In 1983 fast bowler Sean Tracy played for and against the touring New Zealanders in England. The 22-year-old, who was on a county cricket scholarship, opened the bowling for Gloucestershire against the tourists in their second match, at Bristol, taking 2 for 55. Four weeks later he played for the New Zealanders against Hampshire, claiming 2 for 29.

Gerald Hough, an occasional off-break bowler, played in 14 first-class matches for Kent and took his only wicket with his first delivery — against Essex at Leyton in 1919.

Alfred Shaw, who took over 2000 first-class wickets for Nottinghamshire, Sussex and England, had the distinction of clean-bowling W.G. Grace on 20 occasions in first-class cricket. The next most successful at getting through Grace's defences was Tom Richardson, who did him 14 times.

Bowling against Gloucestershire at Nottingham in 1884, Alfred Shaw became the first player to achieve two hat-tricks in the same first-class match. He came close to achieving three, with another burst of three wickets in four balls, an unmatched bowling performance in first-class cricket.

TWO HAT-TRICKS IN THE SAME FIRST-CLASS MATCH

Alfred Shaw	Nottinghamshire v Gloucestershire	Nottingham	1884
Jimmy Matthews	Australia v South Africa	Manchester	1912
Charlie Parker	Gloucestershire v Middlesex	Bristol	1924
'Roley' Jenkins	Worcestershire v Surrey	Worcester	1949
J.S. Rao	Services v Northern Punjab	Amritsar	1963-64
Amin Lakhani	Combined XI v Indians	Multan	1978-79

During the England summer of 1996, Kent bowler Dean Headley claimed a record-equalling three hat-tricks in first-class matches in the season. Charlie Parker of Gloucestershire took two hat-tricks in the same match against Middlesex and one against Surrey in 1924; Indian bowler J.S. Rao took a hat-trick on his first-class debut in 1963-64 and then took another two in his next match.

Headley equalled the world record in the match against Hampshire at Canterbury, which also featured a career-first hat-trick for team-mate Martin McCague, who took five wickets for three in 17 balls.

On the third day of the Karachi Blues-United Bank match at Peshawar in 1994-95 two bowlers achieved hat-tricks. Tauseef Ahmed ended the Karachi innings with three successive wickets, while Ali Gauhar went one better dismissing the first four United Bank batsmen in consecutive balls. In doing so, he became the first Pakistani to achieve the feat of four wickets in four balls in a first-class match, and only the seventh, world-wide, since the Second World War.

A club cricketer from Somerset experienced the ups-and-downs of the game in 1979 when bowling in a match for Curry Rivel v

Pitminster. Brian Rostill had 17 runs taken off his opening eight-ball over, but bounced back in his next, clean-bowling six opposition batsmen.

England spinner Walter Robins and West Indies fast bowler Andy Roberts both took at least one wicket in each of their first 23 innings in Test-match cricket.

During the course of eight consecutive Test-match innings against England in the 1920s, Australia's Clarrie Grimmett seven times conceded over 100 runs, and went for 96 in the other — 3-108 at The Oval in 1926, 3-167 & 6-131 at Brisbane, 2-191 at Sydney, 2-114 & 2-96 at Melbourne and 5-102 & 1-117 at Adelaide in 1928-29.

In 1990-91 Muttiah Muralitharan, from St Anthony's College, became the first Sri Lankan schoolboy to take 100 wickets in two consecutive seasons, a feat that helped propel him into the national side that toured England later in the year.

In the Saravanamutta Trophy of 1994-95, Muralitharan recorded one of first-class cricket's most outstanding analyses — 8 for 8, in 17.3 overs, for Tamil Union v Burgher Recreation Club at Colombo.

A 47-year-old leg-spinner defied the odds in 1985 taking all 10 wickets in an innings in consecutive matches. Representing the Surrey club Shere, Lionel Jones collected 10 for 58 against Hove Montefiore and in his next match, a week later, took 10 for 15.

In his first Test innings against Australia, at Brisbane in 1954-55, England's Frank Tyson produced the unflattering figures of 1 for 160. In the following four Tests he took 27 wickets, including 10 for 130 in the second Test at the SCG.

FRANK TYSON'S 'DREAM TEAM'

Jack Hobbs
Sunil Gavaskar
Don Bradman (c)
Neil Harvey
Denis Compton
Garry Sobers
Don Tallon
Richard Hadlee
Ray Lindwall
Sydney Barnes
Bill O'Reilly

Playing against Australia at Wellington, in 1992-93, Danny Morrison became the first New Zealand bowler to dismiss half-a-dozen batsmen in one session of a Test match. His elimination of Allan Border, Ian Healy, Merv Hughes, Paul Reiffel, Steve Waugh and Shane Warne came in 75 minutes between lunch and tea on the fourth day to give him career-best figures of 7 for 89.

In 1939-40 a Fijian bowler by the name of Saisasi Vunisakiki took eight wickets in a single eight-ball over for Lomaloma v HMS Leith. This was the first time such a feat had been performed in any class of cricket anywhere in the world.

Fast bowler Bruce Reid retired from the first-class game in 1996 with a rare statistical quirk to his credit — the first Australian Test player with 100 wickets to amass more wickets (113) than runs (93). The only other player before him to achieve this unusual Test 'distinction' was India's Bhagwat Chandrasekhar (242 wickets & 167 runs).

In a country cricket match in New South Wales in 1892-93, G. Neale claimed all 10 wickets, for five runs, in an innings, taking three hat-tricks.

Appearing in his first Test match, against New Zealand at Durban in 1961-62, fast bowler Peter Pollock took 6 for 38 in the second innings — his best figures in his 28-match Test career. His match-haul of 9 for 99 was the best by a South African on his Test debut since the War, a record, though, that was broken three weeks later by Sydney Burke, who claimed 11 for 196 in the third Test at Cape Town. In the same Test that Pollock claimed his nine scalps, Frank

Cameron took 6 for 92 (3-60 & 3-32) — the best match-figures by a bowler on his Test debut for New Zealand.

West Indies quick Curtly Ambrose marked his final appearance in Australia with one of the longest overs ever witnessed in Test cricket. In the fifth Test at Perth in 1996-97, Ambrose's final over on Australian soil lasted 12 minutes, 15 balls (nine no-balls) and cost 20 runs. His final fling with the bat also ended in bizarre fashion, when Ian Healy ran him out with an impressive back-handed flick — Ambrose was caught short by a few centimetres when his bat became lodged in a huge crack in the pitch.

QUOTE

"The guy that can throw a really good leg-break is probably a good scientist. I mean, he knows how to do this . . . he may not know the total mechanisms. If he went into the physics of it, he'd be a really good scientist."

— Professor Peter Doherty,
1997 Australian of the Year

MEN IN WHITE COATS

A club cricketer from Nottingham was charged with 'bodily harm by wanton furious driving' in 1992, after he'd reversed his car at an umpire who'd given him out lbw. The batsman was given a suspended sentence and ordered to pay the umpire £400 in compensation.

Dick French, who officiated in 19 Tests and 58 one-day internationals, was the grand-nephew of W.G. French who umpired two Tests in the series between Australia and the West Indies in 1930-31.

In 1995 umpire George Simpson received ten stitches for a head wound after being poleaxed by a ball struck by a batsman during a club match in northern England. Apart from the umpire's displeasure, the batsman — Bishop Auckland's Ricky Waldren — lost his wicket, after the ball rebounded off Simpson's head into the accepting hands of a fieldsman some 45 metres away.

Australia's Steve Randell was on the spot for two of cricket's most highly-publicised ball-tampering incidents. The Tasmanian umpire was officiating at Lord's in 1994 when England captain

> ## QUOTE
> *"I used to worry about what people thought about my umpiring, but I've gotten used to the pressure and I don't care what they think. You live and die by what you do, not what people think you do. And we're just like the players: if we stuff up, we get dropped."*
> — Steve Randell

Mike Atherton was accused of rubbing dirt on a cricket ball, and was also in the middle when Pakistan's Salim Malik accused Zimbabwean umpire Ian Robinson of ball-tampering during the third Test at Harare in 1994-95.

The mild-mannered Randell found himself embroiled in another controversy the following summer, when South African captain Hansie Cronje questioned an umpire's decision during the fifth Test against England at Cape Town.

Standing in only his second Test, Dave Orchard referred a run-out appeal to the third umpire after originally declaring the batsman, Graham Thorpe, had made his ground. After intervention by Cronje, who disputed his opinion, Orchard conferred with Randell, reversed his decision and called for the third umpire's television replay. Thorpe was subsequently given out — Cronje was fined $1250.

QUOTE

"The most difficult type of decisions are the run outs without the assistance of the camera. Progress is essential. If technology assists umpires then it must be used."

— Dave Orchard

During the 1994-95 one-day international series against Australia, a third umpire was used in the West Indies for the first time. One of the umpires in the first match at Bridgetown, however, decided against the use of a television replay to determine a close run-out appeal — a judgment that could have altered the result. Lloyd Barker ruled that Winston Benjamin had made his ground after the stumps were shattered by a direct throw from Greg Blewett. Video replays indicated Benjamin was out, but he stayed on to make another six runs — the final difference between the two teams at the end of the match.

Standing in his second Test match — West Indies v India at Bridgetown in 1952-53 — local umpire Harold Walcott adjudged his nephew, Clyde Walcott, out, lbw, for 98.

After completing the official umpires' course, Carolyn Bowmer, 23, and her father, aged 56, were chosen to officiate together in a match in England's Glossop League competition in 1983.

The father and son of George Hele, who officiated in all five 'Bodyline' Tests in Australia in 1932-33, were also first-class umpires.

Prior to the beginning of the 1990-91 Test series against New Zealand, Pakistan withdrew its offer of neutral umpires following inflammatory remarks allegedly made by the Kiwi captain. Although denied, Martin Crowe was quoted as saying: "We don't anything know about the two guys appointed, but we believe they will be better than having two Pakistani umpires."

A few months after his infamous confrontation with Shakoor Rana during the second Test match at Faisalabad in 1987-88, Mike Gatting bumped into the Pakistani umpire at a one-day match in England.

The Middlesex batsman reportedly refused to speak with Rana, who later expressed his displeasure at being snubbed: "He should have shaken hands, if only for cricket's sake. Then we could have had a cup of tea."

QUOTE

"I am one of Pakistan's most experienced and respected umpires. Cricket has been my life. Now I am an outcast. I am sure even Mr Gatting would not want me to finish up like this."

— Shakoor Rana, on his expulsion from the Pakistan umpires list for failing to undertake a refresher course

"At the time of the row with Mike Gatting I thought Shakoor was in the right in his interpretation of what had happened when he called dead ball. What he did wrong was to seek so much media attention after the incident."

— Imran Khan

Test-umpiring history was made at the MCG in 1995-96, when Darrell Hair controversially called Sri Lanka's Muttiah Muralitharan for throwing. Aware of the spinner's unorthodox and somewhat questionable action, Hair stood back at the bowlers' end and no-balled him seven times, becoming the first umpire in Test history to make such a call at the non-strikers' end.

Although Hair's no-balling of the Sri Lankan guaranteed him a place in the record books, his umpiring had been internationally 'recognised' beforehand. In the three Australian summers that preceded the 1995-96 drama, Hair had each time been the subject of some controversy. At Adelaide in 1992-93, he signalled Craig McDermott out — a decision that gave the West Indies victory by one run. In 1993-94, again at Adelaide, Hair upset the South Africans during the third Test with several controversial lbw decisions and the following season was chastised by the England team for twice failing to consult TV replays for close run-out decisions.

Sri Lanka's outrage at Hair's umpiring during the summer of '95-96 reached boiling point during a World Series match in Perth, with the tourists demanding his replacement for the remainder of their matches.

Darrell Hair has been the unfortunate recipient of several death threats over his umpiring — in South Africa he was a hot topic on talkback radio and the subject of a none-too-kind song, while in Sri Lanka, Hair was lambasted, somewhat cruelly at times, in the national press.

Who is the most patriotic person on earth? Is it Nelson Mandela who languished in jail for 27 years to liberate his people? Or Yitzhak Rabin, who died for the cause of peace?

No my friends, the award goes to a man called Darrell Hair, but I must tell you he had tough competition from two others called Ross Emerson and Steve Randell.

A cardinal principle is that the benefit of the doubt goes to the accused. Once upon a time, all these Aussies were the accused in some cases or the other (ball-tampering, perhaps!) and convicted at the Old Bailey.

The English didn't want them around, so they put them on a ship, giving them the benefit of the doubt, and sent them down under to inhabit a godforsaken continent. But you see, old habits die hard — they still get the benefit of the doubt in an lbw decision.

Meanwhile Mark, you should 'tailor' a new image to cover your moral nakedness. And when you do come to Sri Lanka don't bring that fellow Darrell Hair with you.

There are enough chaps here waiting to no-ball him — though not in the strictly cricketing sense.

— Sri Lanka's *Midweek Mirror* (1996)

Former Indian captain Srinivas Venkataraghavan established a unique record during the 1996 World Cup, becoming the first tournament umpire who had previously appeared in the Cup as a player.

A first-grade Sri Lankan umpire was rebuked by authorities in 1996 after taking a transistor radio onto the field during a match in Colombo. He was listening to descriptions of the Sri Lanka-India World Cup match, and was later reported by players who complained that the noise distracted them.

The cricket ball with which Trevor Chappell bowled the infamous underarm delivery in a one-day international at the MCG in 1980-81 was inadvertently 'souvenired' on the day by a former Test umpire. Dick French, who was there as a spectator, went on to the ground after the match to offer any assistance to the other umpires. He spoke briefly to Don Weser, who admitted it had been a 'tough day'. French replied: "Don't worry about it. Give me the ball and I'll look after it." He did just that, and the ball has remained in his possession ever since.

Eight different umpires stood in the first-class match between Tasmania and Victoria at Launceston in 1908-09. No names, or reasons for the high number, were ever supplied.

Col Egar, one of the umpires in the tied Test at Brisbane in 1960-61, was also an Australian Rules football umpire, who officiated in the South Australian grand finals of 1956 and 1957.

In the final of South Africa's Benson & Hedges one-day tournament at Johannesburg in 1983-84, one of the umpires, Dudley Schoof, claimed to have been hit on the head by, of all things, a frog: "This is certainly the strangest phenomenon that has happened to me on a cricket field and I can only assume that it fell a few hundred feet from the heavy black clouds which were over the ground."

On the eve of his final Test appearance, at Lord's in 1996, 'Dickie' Bird became the first international umpire to be awarded honorary life membership of the MCC.

QUOTE

"I've given everything to cricket. I've never married. I'm married to cricket, you see."

— 'Dickie' Bird

WOMEN AT THE WICKET

QUOTE

"Women's cricket is a game for everybody and we don't care about shape, size, religion or sexual preference. We even have transsexuals playing."

— Ann Mitchell, Australian Women's Cricket Council

The Australian Women's Cricket Council attempted to scrub up its image in 1995, by preparing a code of conduct. The guidelines were rather strict — no gossip, no excessive drinking, no smoking in public view, no swearing publicly or privately, no behaviour that undermines self-esteem, no suggestive gestures, no remarks about a person's looks, etc.

No member shall drink, smoke or gamble while on tour. No girl may be accompanied by her husband, a relation or friend. Writing articles on cricket during the tour is strictly forbidden. While on board ship, no girl shall visit the top deck of the liner after dinner. Members of the team must retire to bed by 10pm during the voyage. Members will do physical drill on deck at 7.15am daily except Sundays. The team will participate in all deck games.

— Australian Women's Cricket Association tour rules for trip to England in 1937

Ten year-old Blair McDowell took a hat-trick in her first over on debut for the New South Wales cricket team, the Seaforth Under-

11s in 1995-96. Blair's remarkable feat was achieved in a team made up mostly of boys.

It was reported in 1993 that the Monica Seles-like grunt of a female cricketer brought about a charge of 'unladylike behaviour'. Oxford's Shamim Umarji was relieved of bowling in a Varsity match for grunting when sending down the ball: "Every time I put 100 per cent into a ball a grunt just slips out."

During the third Test against India at Hyderabad in 1995-96, England's last pair, Debbie Stock and Clare Taylor, batted for over three hours, and 40 overs, to ensure a draw. They both made 9* — Stock faced 142 balls, Taylor 101.

New Zealand's Debbie Hockley, who made her Test debut against Australia in 1978-79 at the age of 16, became national captain when 21 — the youngest Test captain in women's cricket.

During the one-day international series against England in 1996, Hockley scored three consecutive half-centuries — 54 at Lord's, 75 at Leicester and 117, her maiden hundred, at Chester-le-Street. With Shelly Fruin, Hockley shared in two century opening stands — 105 in the first match and a record 150 in the third. In the second Test match at Worcester, Hockley made 115, becoming only the third woman, after England's Enid Bakewell and India's Sandhya Aggarwal, to score four Test hundreds.

During a women's cricket match in Denmark one of the players, who was pregnant, requested a runner complaining of fatigue. The umpire refused, stating that her condition was known before she began the match.

A 17-year-old schoolgirl bowled her male-dominated cricket club to victory in a match in England in 1995 after originally being selected as 12th 'man'. Caroline Lawson, the only female-playing member of the Spofforth Cricket Club, received a late call-up and bowled out the Barwick-in-Elmet team, taking 8 for 40: "I think the opposition was a bit embarrassed because I'm a girl."

In 1996 a 12-year-old girl broke down the barriers when she was chosen to play for a boys' cricket team to tour South Africa. Off-break bowler Laura Harper was granted permission to go when her mother agreed to accompany her on the two-week trip.

During the 1990-91 series between Australia and India, Sandhya Aggarwal took a painstaking 419 minutes to reach her half-century in the first Test at North Sydney. In the second Test, at St Peter's College in Adelaide, India scored 3 for 102 off 101 overs during the course of an entire day's play.

A match in Pakistan in 1996 between women cricketers and veteran male players was abandoned following threats from a leading fundamentalist group. The Jammat-e-Islami Party advised the Pakistan Women's Cricket Control Association of 'dire consequences' if the match proceeded, citing female participation an 'un-Islamic activity'.

In 1994 Clare Tapp, aged 14, became the first female to appear in Buckinghamshire's Midweek League competition. Her first wicket for the Wicken club was caught by her father.

An English women's team, the Maidens of Babbacombe, was forced to cancel its entire cricket schedule in 1985 because four of their top players were pregnant.

New South Wales all-rounder Jo Garey gained selection for the Australian squad in 1996 despite a horrific accident only the year before. Garey nearly lost her right leg in the incident, in which

---

QUOTE

"I was lying on the road and I didn't know what the situation was. I knew I was alive, and I thought, I have just got to play for Australia again."

— Jo Garey

---

another died, after a runaway bus hit her and several others outside a Sydney hotel.

A 15-year-old girl took 10 for 0 from 7.4 overs in a combined Sydney high school cricket carnival in 1995-96. Emma Liddell performed the feat for Seven Hills High School against Metropolitan East, finishing the match with figures of 7.4-7-0-10: "Everyone knew about it by the time I came back to school. Even the guys were impressed, because a lot of them can't understand why a girl would want to play cricket!"

Faith Coulthard (Thomas), known as 'Freight Train', is the only Aborigine to have played Test cricket for Australia. A fast bowler, she appeared in one Test match, against England at St Kilda in 1957-58, in which she failed to take a wicket and scored three runs.

In 1996 New Zealand's Kirsty Flavell scored the first double-century in a women's Test match, hitting 204 against England at Scarborough. Her innings overtook Australian Denise Annetts' previous world-best of 193, scored against England at Collingham in 1987.

History was made in 1996 during the first one-day international between England and New Zealand at Lord's, when women were permitted, for the first time, to watch cricket from the pavilion.

A woman can enter the pavilion during a Test match as a waitress or a queen, but not as a cricket lover. The fact that the club made an exception for the women's one-day international was a small step in the right direction, but hardly a giant leap for womankind. A ban on women is a form of apartheid. The consequences may be trivial, but the principle is the same.

— Editorial, *Wisden Cricket Monthly*

'LE CRICKET'

Just 1150 miles north-east of Sydney lies an Emerald Isle, 250 miles by 31 — New Caledonia. "A tropical paradise of blue waters, white sand, lazy, hot days and balmy evenings", says the travel brochure. Amazingly the brochure goes on to reveal that cricket is played on "this small piece of the South of France with the flavour of Paris." That is unexpected enough, but it becomes quite remarkable when one learns that only the women play. The reason for this seems obscure. It could be that men consider it too 'cissy', but seeing the way in which these tough women play, that seems extremely unlikely.

They are dressed in loose-fitting, gaily coloured floral smocks and the teams are 15-a-side plus two substitutes. The minimum age for a player is fifteen. They were no pads, batting gloves, thigh pads or indeed any other sort of protection so far as one can see under the smocks!

Runs count as in our cricket and are called 'pines', but there are no boundaries and the batswomen must run up and down the pitch barefoot until the ball is returned to the wicket-keeper. It is therefore not surprising that the rules allow for a 'tired' batswoman to be replaced by the next on the list.

The bat must rest on the shoulder and it is forbidden to hold it in the air or to let it touch the ground. If a player drops the bat she must stay in the square until given another one. Incredibly there is only one ball per over, so there is no over-rate problem in New Caledonia!

And now, just in case the whole thing smacks of women's lib, here comes the rub. Both the umpires and the 'off-pitch' scorer must be male. They are considered fairer and have authority in a dispute and are capable of breaking up a scrap if the women get excited and fight — as they often do. Here are some of the general rules these umpires must enforce: it is forbidden for players to throw insults, nor must any player enter the field in a state of drunkenness. Finally, further proof that the umpires are in complete control of the game — neither the players nor the public are allowed to look at the score!

— Brian Johnston, *The Cricketer*

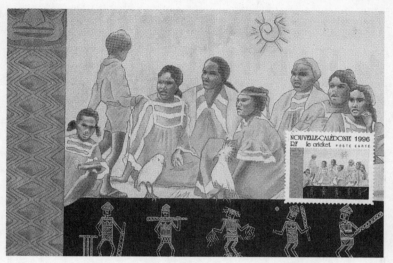

A New Caledonian stamp, celebrating women and cricket, released in 1996

LOVE AND MARRIAGE, SEX AND DIVORCE

> Is it possible that the England team's summer of success in 1985 may be attributed to love? Tim Robinson, Paul Downton, Neil Foster and Richard Ellison have all got married or engaged; John Emburey and Ian Botham's wives both had babies during November; and Graham Gooch's wife is currently pregnant with their second child. Just a thought!
>
> — Letter to the Editor, *Wisden Cricket Monthly* (1986)

> By happy chance, England's two thrilling victories against Australia have fallen either side of the joyous wedding of the Prince and Princess of Wales. What could be more appropriate than to dub these matches 'The Wedding Tests' for posterity?
>
> — Letter to the Editor, *Wisden Cricket Monthly* (1981)

In 1990 England batsman David Gower placed an advertisement in the personal column of *The Times* announcing his separation from his long-time girlfriend: *David Gower and Vicky Stewart would like to put themselves and their friends out of their misery and confirm that sadly they have decided to separate as amicably as possible and go their own ways. As the matter has already been the subject of speculation by some members of the Press, they hope that this brief announcement will obviate the need for further comment. (Fat chance!).*

An upset husband received a £50 fine in 1991 after streaking during the NatWest Bank final at Lord's. Douglas Bruce bared all at the home of cricket, carrying a banner with a proclamation pleading with his wife not to divorce him.

England's Guisborough Cricket Club added an unusual momento to its trophy cabinet in 1996 — a pair of lacy womens' underwear!

While having a drink in their clubhouse, members of the Cleveland team noticed some unusual movement under a protective tarpaulin covering the wicket. When they went to investigate, David Goodchild, the team captain, was confronted with a new definition of lbw — 'legover before wicket': "A couple were going at it hammer and tongs. They were petrified when they saw us, and their first reaction was to cover their faces. Then they grabbed their clothes and sprinted off!"

One piece of clothing, however, was left behind, which was later reserved for the clubhouse. Chairman Dave Normington declared that the woman was free to reclaim the knickers, but added: "Somehow, I doubt she will."

A few days after he was replaced as captain of India in 1996, Mohammad Azharuddin and his wife, Naureen, announced their divorce. During the latter stages of his captaincy, Azharuddin had been accused by the media of 'not being focussed' on the game after a highly-publicised romance with a former Miss India, Sangeeta Bijlani, whom he married a few months following his divorce.

In 1995 India's No.1 batsman Sachin Tendulkar married Anjali Mehta, and turned down a $675,000 offer to have the wedding ceremony televised.

'HIS EYES WERE WILD, PIERCING AND MANIC. HE WAS IN A FRENZY AND COMPLETELY LOST CONTROL' — the headlines in *News of the World* describing former England batsman Geoff Boycott, who was accused of assaulting a 'secret lover' in 1996. The woman, 44-year-old Margaret Moore, claimed that she had

been bashed at a holiday resort in the Riviera: "I was screaming and screaming. It all happened so fast. He had his leg over me really hard. He was punching me over and over with his clenched fist. He was uncontrollable and I was helpless."

After reporting the alleged incident to police, Ms Moore decided against pressing charges, while Boycott denied anything untoward had taken place: "She slipped and fell, hitting the right side of her head on the floor."

> The incident has provided a dramatic insight into 56-year-old Boycott's eventful love-life, which belies his public persona as a dour Yorkshireman. He has reportedly been involved in a number of affairs, including one with a local pub landlady by whom he has a daughter, now 7.
>
> — Steven Morris, *Daily Telegraph*

West Australian batsman Mark Lavender was forced out of the 1991-92 Sheffield Shield final after injuring his ankle in a mysterious accident. It was reported at the time that the opening batsman had hurt himself jumping out of a woman's second-floor window to escape a jealous boyfriend.

A cricket club from Leeds received 30 replies to a newspaper advertisement in 1995 that sought 'fun-loving' women in the Bournemouth area to meet them on their cricket tour.

In 1991 Fred Goodall, a former New Zealand Test umpire, married Di Malthus, a female cricket umpire. The two had met ten years earlier at a cricket match, in which she was playing and he umpiring.

A social cricket match in the Northern Territory in 1980 was interrupted to accommodate a wedding. After a limousine delivered the bride, Anne Thompson, onto the ground, she was escorted down the pitch to join Malcom Wolf where they exchanged their vows: "Anyone can have their wedding in a church or home, but we wanted something a bit different and we were going to the cricket match anyway."

QUOTE

"I love ya Merv."

— Caller to the Triple J radio network, on a same-sex talkback session for Valentine's Day in 1996. The listener also expressed his disappointment that Merv Hughes had failed to respond to his letters.

"One-day cricket is like a quick ejaculation whereas a Test is like amazing long foreplay which may or may not lead to something big."

— Triple J presenter Jaslyn Hall

ALL CREATURES GREAT AND SMALL

A major cricketing milestone was established in Durham in 1995, when a dog retrieved his 500th cricket ball. His owner was regularly contacted by local cricket clubs, eager for the services of Bruce, the Labrador, to search nearby paddocks. A year later, a golden retriever was made an honorary vice-president of a cricket club in Yorkshire, after successfully retrieving 50 lost balls, an effort that saved the club over £1000.

During a country cricket match in Victoria in 1996-97, Damian Glass was dismissed in unusual circumstances — run out, trying to avoid a snake. Opening the batting for Yackandandah against Kiewa, Glass was completing a second run when he was alerted to the intruder, a four-foot brown snake, that had slithered onto the pitch. Taking evasive action, he lost his footing, and was run out.

A three-year-old horse Lash Dem Lara, named after the West Indies batsman Brian Lara, coasted to victory in record time in the 1994 Trinidad Derby. In 1996 a horse named Mr Boone, out of Silly Mid On, came first in a race in Ipswich, while Shane Warne, a four-year-old bay colt, won the '96 Pakistan Derby.

In 1988 Ian Botham beat the world fly-fishing champion in a charity competition in England, by hauling in an 18lb 12oz trout.

Blair Sellers was denied a century in an under-16 competition in 1994-95, thanks to a seagull. During his innings for the South Melbourne club, a shot that was set to go the boundary hit a bird in flight, turning four runs into just two. He was eventually out for 98.

Play was brought to a halt during the England-Pakistan Test match at Edgbaston in 1962 when a mouse came on to the field!

In 1995 a Welsh cricket team was forced to run chook raffles to raise money for the purchase of balls confiscated by a resident who lived on the edge of their village green. Concerned by the possibility that children could get hit in her backyard by wayward sixes, Suzie Rich refused to return any balls hit in her garden until they provided a bigger fence.

There was much mayhem in the match between the MCC and Yorkshire at Scarborough in 1892, when an out-of-control horse and cart careered onto the pitch.

A tightly-contested match between two junior teams in Sydney in 1996-97 was interrupted when a parrot 'buzzed' the ground. After circling the pitch at high speed, the colourful bird quietly settled on the shoulder of the umpire at the bowlers' end. Unperturbed, the umpire allowed the over to be completed before several fielders gently escorted the intruder from the field of play.

A cricket match in Lancashire in 1995 was brought to a halt when a dog, owned by one of the players, was found chasing a herd of cows in an adjoining paddock. Things were made worse when the farmer started chasing the dog, followed by the dog's owner chasing the farmer!

KEEPING UP
APPEARANCES

When Lancashire played Leicestershire in the County Championship match at Old Trafford in 1996, the only batsmen to score centuries were the wicket-keepers. Warren Hegg made 134 for Lancashire, while Paul Nixon hit 106 for Leicestershire.

In 1975 a unique instance of wicket-keepers scoring centuries while opening the batting took place at Taunton, with Mike Harris making 163 for Nottinghamshire, and Derek Taylor 127 for Somerset.

When the Australian Young Cricketers toured England in 1983, Ian Healy played in two 'Test' matches as a batsman. The wicket-keeper was the junior Australian rugby league player Bronko Djura.

During a club match against Enfield in England in 1987, Loughton wicket-keeper Simon Fitzgerald picked up five stumpings off the bowling of Martin Figg (5-50). The bowler ended the innings with an all-stumped hat-trick.

In a Minor Counties match against Wales at Bletchley in 1988, Buckinghamshire wicket-keeper Colin Tungate took seven catches in an innings off the bowling of Chris Booden.

In 1984 Neil Burns made eight stumpings, three in the first innings and five in the second, for the Essex 2nd XI against Kent at Dartford.

In the first Test against England at Manchester in 1950, the West Indies' wicket-keeper/batsman Clyde Walcott made history by opening the bowling (4-1-12-0) in the second innings. He filled in for an injured Hines Johnson, while Robert Christiani stood behind the stumps.

After scoring his maiden first-class century (148) in 1996-97, Victoria's Darren Berry gloved an Australian-record eight dismissals in an innings in his next match, against South Australia. His counterpart in this game, Tim Nielsen, also created history by batting for 69 minutes without scoring a run in the second innings — a record in a first-class match at the Melbourne Cricket Ground.

One of cricket's most remarkable all-round performances was achieved by a wicket-keeper in Zimbabwe in 1995-96 when Wayne James broke a major record behind the stumps and backed it up with a heart-breaking double with the bat.

Playing against Mashonaland Country Districts in the Logan Cup final at Bulawayo, Matebeleland's captain and wicket-keeper achieved nine dismissals in the first innings, to equal the world record, and then picked up another four victims in the second. His 13 dismissals represented a new international record in first-class cricket, beating the 12 snared by Surrey's Ted Pooley in 1868 (v Sussex at The Oval), Queensland's Don Tallon in 1938-39 (v New South Wales at Sydney) and NSW's Brian Taber in 1968-69 (v South Australia at Adelaide).

He also became one of the game's unluckiest batsmen, failing by one run in each innings to score a century (99 & 99*): "I didn't realise my score in the first innings, because the full scoreboard wasn't in operation, but I knew all right in the second. We needed three to win, and the plan was for my partner Mark Dekker to push a single and give me the strike. But you don't get first-class hundreds that easily, and the bowler pushed one down the leg side and the "keeper missed it. It might just have been deliberate . . . but it didn't matter. The main thing was that we won the Logan Cup."

England's Alec Stewart was the top-scoring batsman in Test matches in the calendar year of 1996, with a total of 793 runs at an average of 61. His aggregate was boosted by an innings by 101* achieved on the penultimate day of the year, against Zimbabwe at Harare — his first hundred for England as wicket-keeper. Stewart then scored another hundred (173) in his next match, against New Zealand at Auckland, becoming the first England 'keeper to pass 150 in a Test.

In 1996-97 Ian Healy became the first Queensland-born cricketer to score a Test century at the 'Gabba. His unbeaten 161 in the first Test against the West Indies was the highest innings by an Australian wicket-keeper in a Test and he became the first player in history to have scored his first three first-class centuries in Test matches. His previous two hundreds were 102* against England at Manchester in 1993 and 113* against New Zealand in Perth five months later.

HIGHEST TEST SCORES BY WICKET-KEEPERS

210*	Taslim Arif	Pakistan v Australia	Faisalabad	1979-80
209	Imtiaz Ahmed	Pakistan v New Zealand	Lahore	1955-56
201*	Brendon Kuruppu	Sri Lanka v New Zealand	Colombo	1986-87
192	'Budhi' Kunderan	India v England	Madras	1963-64
182	Denis Lindsay	South Africa v Australia	Johannesburg	1966-67
173	Ian Smith	New Zealand v India	Auckland	1989-90
173	Alec Stewart	England v New Zealand	Auckland	1996-97
168*	Clyde Walcott	West Indies v England	Lord's	1950
161*	Ian Healy	Australia v West Indies	Brisbane	1996-97

James Didcote, a slow bowler with the Glamorgan Colts side, was no-balled on two occasions in a match against Llandovery College in 1995, under Law 40.1 ('The wicket-keeper shall remain wholly behind the wicket until a ball delivered by the bowler touches the bat or person of the striker, or passes the wicket, or until the striker attempts a run'). The offending wicket-keeper was Gareth Jones, the son of former Glamorgan 'keeper Eifion Jones, whose cap had protruded in front of the stumps while Didcote was delivering the ball.

The first Test match between New Zealand and Zimbabwe at Hamilton in 1995-96 provided the first instance in Test history of wicket-keeper/captains — Lee Germon and Andy Flower — opposing each other.

Somerset's Derek Taylor took a world-record eight catches in the Benson & Hedges one-day match against Oxford & Cambridge Universities at Taunton in 1982.

CRICKET AND POLITICS

Alf Stafford, who played grade cricket in Sydney and captained the ACT against the New South Wales Sheffield Shield team in 1935-36, later became the official car driver for various Prime Ministers, including the cricket-loving Bob Menzies, John Curtin and Ben Chifley.

Who is this man, with creaking bones, This ancient, uttering oaths and groans, Bowling round-arms, and that most vilely? Sir, 'tis the ghost of Bill O'Reilly.

— Sir Robert Menzies

QUOTE

"Cricket is a game not only of skill but of character. It is not something to be hustled through. It requires time, the setting and the delicacies of art to achieve its full expression. That is why every great cricketer is not only a member of a team but an individual endowed with the fascinating faculty of conveying by bat or ball or gesture his personality, far across the distant ropes or pickets and into the very hearts and minds of the spectators."

"If the art of cricket is to survive, many people must contribute to the survival. The spectator naturally loves a good swiping innings, with a few sixes thrown in, but he must also have time and intelligence to admire the artistry of non-scoring defence against aggressive and shrewd bowling."

— Sir Robert Menzies

Charles Williams, who scored over 4000 first-class runs for Oxford University and Essex in the 1950s, later entered politics, rising to the position of deputy leader of the Labour opposition. Williams is also an author of some note; his first book — *The Last Great Frenchman* — an acclaimed biography of French President Charles de Gaulle.

Frank Nicklin, who was Premier of Queensland between 1957 and 1968, played as a batsman for a Queensland Country XI team in 1928-29. Jack Pizzey, who succeeded Nicklin as Premier, was also a cricketer of some note — his only chance of playing the first-class game ruined by rain. He had been selected to appear in the match between Queensland and Victoria at the 'Gabba in 1930-31 — the first of only three Sheffield Shield matches to be abandoned without a ball bowled.

Cricket received a special mention in a major speech in the House of Commons in 1996. Delivering the budget, the Chancellor Kenneth Clarke revealed that Britain's income-tax rate was at its lowest level in sixty years, when "Baldwin was Prime Minister, Edward VIII abdicated and Wally Hammond scored a double-century at The Oval."

C.B. Fry, the former England Test captain who had gained considerable expertise in the training and education of young men, was once sent for by Adolf Hitler, to assist the Nazi Party in the establishment of its Youth Movement.

During the 1920s, Fry stood three times, unsuccessfully, for Parliament representing the Liberal Party (Hove in 1922, Banbury in 1923 and Oxford in 1924).

In 1997 Australia's Industrial Relations Minister Peter Reith made an appearance in a charity cricket match between the Liberal Party's 500 Club and Lords Taverners in Melbourne, but was forced to retire hurt on 16 with a hamstring injury. Former Australian cricket captain Graham Yallop made 45.

> ## QUOTE
> *"I always like playing on a sticky wicket."*
> — Former Prime Minister, Paul Keating

During his term as Prime Minister, Paul Keating employed the occasional cricketing analogy, but came unstuck in 1995, when he described his fondness for hitting for six, anything put to him by the Liberal Party, into the Queen Elizabeth Stand. John Howard, who, at the time, was Leader of the Opposition, was quick to point out that no such stand existed at an Australian cricket ground — it's at the Randwick race course.

During the 1996 federal election campaign, Mr Howard was also caught out, when he proudly boasted that Test cricketer Mark Waugh was a constituent of his Sydney-based seat of Bennelong. He got it wrong — at the time, Waugh was enrolled in the Labor-held seat of Banks.

Kim Beazley, the Federal Opposition Leader, once took a hat-trick in a district cricket match, and was given the ball to prove it. Representing the Claremont-Cottesloe fourth-grade club in a match at North Fremantle Oval in 1965, Beazley took 8 for 30, including the hat-trick, but finished on the losing side. The hat-trick ball was presented to the young Beazley at the end of the match by one Graham McKenzie, the Australian fast bowler, who was present at the ground.

On the day that Gough Whitlam was dismissed as Prime Minister — 11 November 1975 — Western Australia's Terry Alderman was dismissed for a duck in the Sheffield Shield match against Queensland in Perth.

KIM BEAZLEY'S 'DREAM TEAM'

Len Hutton
Bill Ponsford
Don Bradman (c)
Walter Hammond
George Headley
Graeme Pollock
Garry Sobers
Godfrey Evans
Bill O'Reilly
Dennis Lillee
Andy Roberts

Sri Lanka's 1996 World Cup-winning captain Arjuna Ranatunga comes from a family seemingly devoted to both cricket and politics. Three of his brothers have played Test or one-day international cricket, while another entered parliament, becoming a Minister in Sri Lanka's Western Provincial Government. Arjuna's father, Reggie Ranatunga, is also a politician — a Minister in the People's Alliance Government.

George Reid, Australia's Prime Minister from 1904 to 1905, was, at the same time, the President of the New South Wales Cricket Association.

England's retention of the 'Ashes' reminds me of a curious but little-known statistic. Since the war the Conservative and Labour parties have held power for roughly equal lengths of time (18 years 11 months and 17 years 4 months respectively). During the same period England has held the 'Ashes' for 13½ years: of these, 10¾ years (with more to come) have been during Conservative governments, but only 2¾ under Labour. Cricket-loving patriots will know which way to vote next time!

— Letter to the Editor, *The Times* (1981)

Cricketing metaphors are without a doubt perfectly intelligible to English readers who play the game, but are they to the Russians, who do not? What, for example, do they make of the following extract from your leading article on 11 March:

(Mr Khrushchev) "feels himself free to lob ideas on Berlin and Germany because he has done most of the bowling since his Note of November 27 and the West — apart from Mr Macmillan's appearance in Moscow — has been stonewalling."

— Letter to the Editor, *The Times* (1959)

Indian police claimed in 1996 to have foiled an attempt to kidnap former Indian cricket captain Kapil Dev. The chief of police in Punjab revealed that up to five members of a separatist political group had planned to kidnap and hold the cricket star hostage to promote their cause of independence for Kashmir.

Sir Henry Harben, President of the Sussex County Cricket Club in 1901 and 1906, was a cousin of British politician Joseph Chamberlain.

John Howard, the bowler

> **QUOTE**
>
> *"Sport and politics are two great passions. I retain to this day an absolute passion for cricket."*
>
> — John Howard

One of the Prime Minister John Howard's most cherished childhood memories is the day his father took him to his first big cricket match — one that was attended by the Prime Minister of the day, Ben Chifley. It was the Oldfield-Kippax Testimonial Match at the SCG in 1948-49, where Don Bradman, in his penultimate first-class appearance, made 53.

Mr Howard describes himself as an 'average' cricketer — he made the 2nd XI at Canterbury Boys' High School in Sydney and also played with the Earlwood Methodists team in the New South Wales Churches competition: "Six for 57 was my best, against St Cuthberts, South Kogarah. I still remember it."

England's Conservative Party revealed in 1995 that ten thousand people a week had visited a page on the Internet to play a cricket game — the object of which was to place a ball near a bat held by the Prime Minister of the day, John Major.

> **QUOTE**
>
> *"As a youngster, I dreamt of playing for my country and would willingly have traded high office for just one appearance against Australia at The Oval. In the next life, I shall bowl . . . and hope."*
>
> — John Major

When US President Bill Clinton visited the Queensland centre of Port Douglas in 1996 one of those who lined up to greet him was the president of the local cricket club. After welcoming the US leader, he respectfully requested if his helicopters would not land on the cricket pitch.

Henry Mulholland, Speaker of Northern Ireland's House of Commons from 1929 to 1945, played first-class cricket for Ireland and Cambridge University (1911-14).

John Taylor, England's first black Conservative peer, entered the House of Lords in 1996. Among his first words in the chamber ... "My father, Derief Taylor, was a cricketer for Warwickshire in the 1940s and '50s and it was his ambition for me to play at Lord's. But I'm sure he would settle for this."

All-rounder Manoj Prabhakar contested, unsuccessfully, India's general election in 1996 as a candidate for a rival faction of the then Prime Minister Narasimha Rao's Congress Party. His decision to seek political office was in protest at his exclusion from the Indian cricket team: "I need some platform to raise my voice against the injustice done to me." Prabhakar's election campaign was officially launched by former captain and team-mate Kapil Dev.

Q: "You're an angry man aren't you?"
A: "I was an angry man. If somebody is nice to me, I'll be nice to him. If somebody acts funny, I will be the same."
Q: "You'd concede, though, that being a politician means more than bowling an outswinger?"
A: "In politics you have to bowl not an outswinger or inswinger ... you have to bowl a googly. Because if you show your action ... plan of action ... then they will come to know what you're going to do. I'm not showing any action. I'm just playing my own way."

— Interview with Manoj Prabhakar, ABC Radio

In the same election, Chetan Chauhan, the former Indian Test opener, lost the Amroha seat that he'd held since 1991.

'Doc' Evatt, the leader of the Australian Labor Party between 1951 and 1960, captained his school cricket team in Sydney and played for the 2nd XI at Sydney University. Evatt's love of the game was lifelong, becoming a vice-president of the New South Wales Cricket Association, Australia's delegate to the Imperial Cricket Conference in 1938 and patron, for 22 years, of the Balmain cricket club in Sydney.

Cheryl Kernot, the leader of the Australian Democrats, joined Darrell Hair as an umpire in a celebrity cricket match in Sydney in 1996-97 to launch the Women's National Cricket League.

QUOTE

"The laws of cricket are written down, players have to abide by them and when you're out, you're out. It's not quite the same in politics."

— Cheryl Kernot

Abraham Lincoln, who would later become President of the United States, was a spectator at a cricket match between Chicago and Milwaukee in 1849.

In 1965 US Secretary of State Dean Rusk made the headlines in Washington when he attended a cricket match on the day that celebrated Jamaica's independence.

QUOTE

"I'm very grateful that I grew up in a world that had cricket. It's given me great enjoyment and excitement. All vicariously, of course: I would have made the world's worst cricketer if I had ever concentrated on it."

— Michael Manley, Prime Minister of Jamaica
(1972-80)

During a dispute involving open-cast mining in England in 1995, an unusual protest was staged in the garden of the deputy Prime Minister's Northamptonshire home. An impromptu cricket match, in which coal shovels were used as bats, was played before the protesters dispersed.

Following Pakistan's defeat at the hands of India in the 1996 World Cup, the government of the day, led by Benazir Bhutto, suggested an inquiry be launched into the causes of the loss. The offer was made in the Pakistan Senate where opposition members heaped scorn on the government for the national humiliation caused by the country's arch-rivals.

QUOTE
"Any nation which made a woman its ruler never prospered."

— Mulsim religious cleric Maulana Naqshbandi,
referring to the then Prime Minister Benazir Bhutto,
after Pakistan's exit from the 1996 World Cup

Up until 1985-86 one of South Australia's long-standing partnership records was held by a West Indies captain and a federal politician. In 1963-64 Garry Sobers and Defence Minister Ian McLachlan shared a record 253-run stand for the fourth wicket against the touring South Africans.

During a Parliamentary session in 1996, Mr McLachlan was accused of 'stonewalling' in answer to a question from the Opposition. Gavan O'Connor, the member for Corio, interjected during the Minister's reply in Question Time: "He thinks he's opening against the West Indies!" The former South Australian and Cambridge University batsman replied that he had done just that: "I point out that the important thing to remember when they are bowling bouncers, is to make sure your back foot does not move towards the square-leg umpire."

QUOTE

*"Bradman put a slide up on a projector, a black and white of
a left-arm bowler obviously throwing in the delivery stride.
He said 'who's that?' and no one got it. Not Richie
(Benaud), no one. It was Harold Larwood reversed. Quite an
interesting night. But the throwers had a big advantage anyway. I used to do it in the nets, and just by bending my arm
a little . . . boy! I could generate a whole lot of extra pace."*

— Ian McLachlan

Mike Whitney, the former Australian fast bowler and a card-carry-
ing member of the Labor Party, has been courted by successive
Premiers of New South Wales, eager to gain his services at
Macquarie Street. Both the Liberal Party's Nick Greiner and the
ALP's Bob Carr assured Whitney of a bright future in politics:
"Bob Carr has mentioned it to me a couple of times. But it's got
to be the worst job in the world. I met Nick Greiner at a turnout
and he said he would like to have a meeting. When his secretary
rang me, I asked if Nick knew I was a member of the Labor Party.
She said she'd have to get back to me and never did!"

When the cricket match between members of NSW and
Vic. Parliaments was played in Melbourne recently, a
spectator said to a prominent cricketer who was also
watching the game: "Don't you think any average cricketer would make as good a member of Parliament as any
of those fellows?" "My oath!" remarked the P.C. "Well,
how is it that they play such poor cricket?" enquired the
other. "That's a different thing," replied the P.C. gravely;
"to play cricket properly a man must have brains, and
judgement, and training."

— *The Bulletin*, 13 February 1897

Robin Marlar, who appeared in over 200 first-class matches for Sussex in the 1950s and '60s, stood as an independent candidate, on an Anti-Maastricht Treaty ticket, in a 1993 by-election in Newbury. Marlar had previously contested political office, in 1959 and 1962.

South African President Nelson Mandela was patron of the 1997 benefit fund for England fast bowler Devon Malcolm.

QUOTE

"I know you. You are the destroyer."

— South African President Nelson Mandela, on meeting Devon Malcolm who took 9 for 57 against the South Africans at The Oval in 1994

Abdul Kardar, who captained Pakistan in the 1950s, studied economics, philosophy and politics at Oxford University, where, he said, he learned "to take up causes and remain firm in matters of national importance." Between 1970 and 1977 Kardar was a member of the Punjab Provincial Assembly, serving some time as Education Minister.

TED MACK'S 'DREAM TEAM'

Jack Hobbs
Len Hutton
Don Bradman (c)
Walter Hammond
Viv Richards
Garry Sobers
Keith Miller
Don Tallon
Ray Lindwall
Bill O'Reilly
Clarrie Grimmett

During the Australian federal election campaign of 1996, Joe Hockey, the Liberal candidate for the seat of North Sydney, highlighted his background in fighting local state-based issues. He said his civic interests began at the age of 14, when he successfully campaigned for new cricket nets in the Sydney suburb of Northbridge. Mr Hockey succeeded the retiring Independent member, Ted Mack.

BOB HAWKE — FIRST-GRADE CRICKETER AND PRIME MINISTER

"There was a prize of a bat for anyone in the First XI who could make 100 runs in a final-year game. In the five years I'd been at Mod nobody had won the bat. The match came, and I'd made 93 runs and I thought, 'This is it! I'm going to crack the record!' I knew how proud dad would be if I won it. Then Cyril Calcutt, who taught maths-science, bowled a ball that pitched outside the leg stump, and I went to hook the thing and was given out LBW. There was no way in the world I was out! By God, I was so annoyed. I was enormously disappointed. It was, really, one of the biggest disappointments of my schooldays. . . One of my only real regrets is that I didn't learn to bat well until I went to Oxford and had coaching. If only I could have learned when I was younger."

Apocryphal stories were circulating about Hawke on campus. One was that when not selected for the first-grade cricket team he had called a meeting, stacked it, had the selectors dismissed and installed new ones who promptly selected him.

A university friend said, "One day he came to a cricket match, wearing shorts, and sat stroking his leg, looking at it as if he loved it. He was a narcissist."

— From *Robert J. Hawke: A Biography* by Blanche d'Alpuget

In a cabinet reshuffle in 1981, Neil Macfarlane was made Minister of Sport in the government of Margaret Thatcher. Mr Macfarlane, an MCC member, played cricket in the 1950s for Essex Young Amateurs.

JOHN FAHEY'S 'DREAM TEAM'

Mark Taylor
Geoff Boycott
Viv Richards
Don Bradman (c)
Steve Waugh
Clive Lloyd
Rod Marsh
Shane Warne
Imran Khan
Alan Davidson
Dennis Lillee

John Fahey — Federal Finance Minister and former New South Wales Premier

Upon the outbreak of renewed hostilities between Pakistan and India in 1965 a team of international cricketers, playing in England, sent a joint telegram to the Indian Prime Minister and Pakistani President: *We world cricket team wish express deep regrets at declared war between India, Pakistan. Coming from different countries, backgrounds, races, religions, we find unity on cricket field by reaching for common objective. Fervently hope both countries can meet and find amicable solution.*

Lord Dalmeny, who played first-class cricket for Middlesex, Surrey and Scotland during the early 1900s, was the son of Lord Rosebery, who succeeded William Gladstone as British Prime Minister in 1894. In 164 first-class innings, he made 3551 runs at 22.47, with a top score of 138.

ROSEMARY CROWLEY'S 'DREAM TEAM'

Bill Lawry
Gordon Greenidge
Garry Sobers
Don Bradman (c)
Viv Richards
Steve Waugh
Rod Marsh
Dennis Lillee
Ray Lindwall
Shane Warne
Derek Underwood

Rosemary Crowley — South Australian Labor senator and former Family Services Minister

QUOTE

"One of my favourite cricket memories: Our family was driving from Adelaide to Canberra, over-nighting at Tallangatta on our way through. It was coming on to close of play as we approached the town and Dougie Walters was playing superbly as only he could. The question was could he make a century in a session. As we reached the motel, it was touch and go. We leapt from the car and raced into the motel. 'Where's the TV,' we yelled, found it just in time and saw Dougie hit a six for his century in the session. Hurrahs!!! Hat's off!!! Cheers!!! Then we drew a deep breath, collected our luggage and checked in. A perfect end to a splendid family day in Australia's countryside."

— Rosemary Crowley

Imran Khan, who launched his own political party to fight corruption, failed to sway the nation's voters when he sought the prime ministership in Pakistan's general election of 1997. His Justice Movement did not gain a single seat in the 217-seat National Assembly, in an election that was resoundingly won by Nawiz Sharif's Pakistan Muslim League.

Despite the setback Imran vowed to continue his fight, claiming he had successfully positioned his movement for future success: "We will now struggle afresh to strengthen and develop our party."

ALL IN THE FAMILY

In a first-class match between The Rest and the Hindus at Bombay in 1943-44, Vijay Hazare contributed handsomely with an innings of 309. The next highest individual score for The Rest was just 21, by his brother Vivek. Batting together they put on 300 for the sixth wicket.

At The Oval in 1983, Jeff and Martin Crowe became the fifth pair of brothers to play together in the same Test match for New Zealand. They marked their appearance by both scoring a duck in the first innings.

Two fathers-and-sons performed with unusual distinction in a club match in England in 1989 — one pair starring with the bat, the other the ball.

Captaining the Potters Bar Extra 3rd XI, Tony Rainsborough scored 52, while his son made 101*. Bowling unchanged, Alan and Mark Cooke then disposed of the Northampton Exiles for 68, the father taking 5 for 31, the son 5 for 32.

On 11 July 1990 two brothers made matching innings of 103. Keith Brown scored his century for Middlesex against Surrey in the NatWest Trophy — Gary Brown's 103* was scored for Minor Counties v the touring Indians at Trowbridge.

Another same-day fraternal feat was recorded in 1992, when William and Andrew Sharp scored their maiden hundreds in senior-grade cricket for the Manchester club Grappenhall. William made 114* for the 1st XI, while his brother Andrew hit a neat 100 for the 3rd XI.

Bernard Tyler, who played first-class cricket for Leicestershire and Northants in the 1920s, once had the distinction of appearing in a match for the Oakham Town club with his father, Ralph, and son, Ray.

The father of Patrick Eagar, the world-famous cricket photographer, was a proficient batsman who played for Oxford, Gloucestershire and Hampshire. In over 300 first-class matches stretching from 1935 to 1957, Ted Eagar scored 12,178 runs at 21.86, topping 1000 runs in a season six times.

Four brothers played alongside another set of brothers in the Middlesex-Surrey match at the Oval in 1862. The visitors' line-up included A.H., I.D., R.D. and V.E. Walker and G. and T. Hearne. Two years later, at Hove, the Middlesex side playing Sussex included G. and T. Hearne, plus another mixture of brothers from the Walker clan — I.D., J., R.D. and V.E.

Two sets of twins from the same family tried their luck at selection trials for the Cleveland Schools under-13 squad in England in 1996 — Alex and Lee Roberts, aged 13, and 12-year-old brothers Jay and Brett. Only Jay failed to make it.

In 1995-96 South African fast bowler Shaun Pollock played in a World XI team against the Australians at the MCG. The last time a World XI appeared in Australia was in 1971-72 — in the squad was Shaun's father, Peter, and uncle, Graeme.

Apart from Shaun's famous Test-playing father and uncle, two of his cousins — Anthony and Andrew Pollock — play for Transvaal, while a grandfather kept wicket for Orange Free State.

The fastest century scored in domestic cricket in Sri Lanka in 1994-95 came off the bat of Arjuna Ranatunga, who reached three figures off 98 balls in 123 minutes (107 for Sinhalese SC v Sebastianites). The slowest hundred of the season was scored by his brother Sanjeeva, whose 124 lasted 508 minutes and 371 balls (Nondescripts v Bloomfield). Both hundreds were scored at the Maitland Place ground in Colombo.

In 1995 Zimbabwean batsman Grant Flower, playing for Barnt Green, became only the tenth batsman in England's Birmingham League to score 1000 runs in a season. A week earlier, his brother Andy had became the ninth to achieve the feat, playing for West

Bromwich Dartmouth.

On hand for the Worcestershire-Oxford match at The Parks in 1996, journalist Ralph Dellor found himself acting as 12th man for the home-side. The 12th man for Worcestershire was his son.

At Bristol in 1868, W.G. Grace and his brother G.F. took all 20 wickets for Clifton against Gloucester. In 1889 W.G. and another brother, E.M., representing Thornbury, bowled out Wotton-under-Edge for 35 and eight, each taking 10 wickets.

The first century in Test-match cricket was scored by Australian opening batsman Charles Bannerman (165*), against England at Melbourne in 1876-77. His brother, Alec, also an opener, scored the first Test ninety — 94 v England at Sydney in 1882-83.

In a County Championship match at Northampton in 1975, Leicestershire's John Steele took the most wickets (9), while his brother David, appearing for Northants, scored the most runs (46 & 60).

In 1995-96 a 46-year-old Denis Streak — who had last played first-class cricket on Zimbabwe's England tour in 1985 — was drafted into the Matabeland XI, that included his son Heath, for the Logan Cup final against Mashonaland.

On the New South Wales South Coast in 1975-76, Barry Jennings (104*) and his son, Mark (110*), both scored unbeaten centuries in the same innings for the Berry 3rd XI against Kangaroo Valley.

The captain of Pakistan's squad in the Under-15 World Cup, played in England in 1996, was Faisal Iqbal, a nephew of former Test skipper Javed Miandad. Imran Qadir, the son of leg-spinner Abdul Qadir was also in the team, as was Majid Khan's son, Bazid.

Playing for Yorkshire club Bradley in 1993, twin brothers James and Simon Heseltine both scored 24* against Conorley.

When Oxford University played at The Oval in 1983, Surrey's wicket-keeper Alec Stewart was joined on the field by his father, Micky, who acted as a substitute. This was the first occasion the two had taken part in the same first-class match, during the course of which Alec scored his maiden century (118*).

During the second Test at Melbourne in 1882-83, Australia's George Giffen became a part of history when he was dismissed for a duck by Billy Bates, forming part of the first-ever Test-match hat-trick by an England bowler. Giffen's brother, Walter, was one of the three victims of the next England hat-trick against Australia, at Sydney in 1891-92.

On his first-class debut for Hampshire, against Middlesex, in 1996, Liam Botham, the son of Ian, made headlines by taking 5 for 67 in 15 overs. His first wicket, achieved with his seventh ball, was that of his father's former England team-mate, Mike Gatting.

Kent's Dean Headley made history in 1996 when he made his one-day international debut for England, becoming the first third-gerneration player from the same family to be chosen for his country. The fast bowler followed in the footsteps of his father, Ron, and grandfather, George, who both played Test cricket for the West Indies.

In the same match that Dean made his debut — the first one-day international against Pakistan at Manchester — two other players with family connections were also blooded. Lancashire batsman Graham Lloyd, who began his international career with a score of 2*, is the son of former England Test cricketer David. The other debutant was the Melbourne-born all-rounder Adam Hollioake, whose brother, Ben, made his Surrey first-class debut earlier in the season.

In the County Championship match against Sussex at Worcester in 1996, brothers Keith and Mike Newell were both run out in consecutive overs by Keith Greenfield. Mike completed a pair on his first-class debut.

The father of Test star Mike Procter played for Eastern Province against the MCC side captained by Walter Hammond in 1938-39. Mike and his brother, Anton, played together on a number of occasions for Natal in the Currie Cup.

Playing for the Lancashire 2nd XI in 1996, Patrick McKeown and Nathan Wood opened against Kent at Canterbury with a record first-wicket stand of 341. The previous best was 266 by Nathan's father, Barry Wood, and John Abrahams against Warwickshire in 1975.

In a village cricket match in England in 1922, Sidney Causton took six wickets in six balls for Mundford. Seventy-four years later, in 1996, his great-grandson, Nick, aged 14, performed the same feat for the Brooke's under-18 XI v Loddon in the Norfolk Youth League.

Former television football commentator Graeme Hughes and his two brothers, Garry and Mark, played first-grade cricket together for the Petersham club in Sydney. Graeme appeared in 20 first-class matches for New South Wales in the 1970s, while his father, Noel, played in 21 matches for Worcestershire in the 1950s.

When Australia and Kenya met for the first time in a one-day international, at the 1996 World Cup, three sets of brothers were on display — Steve and Mark Waugh, Maurice and Edward Odumbe and Steve and David Tikolo.

History was made in 1996-97 when Zimbabwe included three sets of brothers in its squad that toured Pakistan — Grant and Andy Flower, Paul and Bryan Strang and Gavin and John Rennie. A pair of cousins, Guy and Andy Whittall, also made the trip.

Brett Swain, a medium-fast bowler who made his first-class debut for South Australia in 1995-96, is a grandson of 'Tim' Wall, the bowler who topped the Australian averages in the 1932-33 'Bodyline' Test series against England.

The two highest run-scorers in Test-match cricket during the 1970s were brothers-in-law. India's Sunil Gavaskar and Gundappa Viswanath both played in 108 innings during the decade — the former scoring 5647 runs, the latter 4611.

In 1992-93 brothers Mark (224) and John (203*) Lane both scored double-centuries in an opening partnership of 393 for their club Marlborough (1d-461) against Buller in New Zealand's U-Bix Cup.

John Stuart, the father of New South Wales fast bowler Anthony Stuart, took the first-ever wicket for the Newcastle cricket club Charlestown in the 1960s.

Brian Mundin, a bowler with the Ibis cricket club in England, and his son, Phillip, both claimed a hat-trick on the same day in 1987. The father took his three-in-three against Galgate, while his son claimed 5 for 3, and the hat-trick, in an under-15s match.

An unusual fraternal partnership blossomed in a country cricket match in Victoria in 1956, when brothers Ted and Claude Cooper were the only players required to bat in a match against Katamatite. Opening the innings for Barooga, Ted scored 110* and Claude 61* in a first-wicket partnership of 0 declared for 171. After the opposition had been dismissed for 117, Ted (39*) and Claude (25*) replied with 0 declared for 66 in Barooga's second innings.

WHAT'S IN A NAME?

Remembering that a former Nottinghamshire wicket-keeper was named Oates, I notice with interest that the present occupant of the position is Wheat. It recalls my youthful glee to find Root following Beet on the Derbyshire card years ago, and, more recently, that the Surrey team included both Hobbs and Fender.

— Letter to the Editor, *The Times* (1937)

During the two-match Test series against the West Indies in 1995-96, New Zealand's number two batsman, the appropriately-named Roger Twose, scored 2, 2, 0 and 2.

On his Test debut for Australia, at Karachi in 1982-83, Greg Ritchie was dismissed by two bowlers whose names began with the letter Q — Abdul Qadir and Iqbal Qasim.

In Pakistan in 1994-95, Australian fast bowler Glenn McGrath's name appeared as 'MAC GROT' on a cricket-ground scoreboard. And in the West Indies a few months later, Greg Blewett's name appeared as 'BLEWIES' on the scoreboard at Sabina Park.

Several comical spelling blunders emerged during the 1996 World Cup — 'MICHEL ARTHERTON', for Mike Atherton and 'P. STRANGE', for Zimbabwe's Paul Strang.

When Victorian batsman Wayne Phillips made his Test debut in 1991-92, he became the second player of that name to represent Australia.

Some confusion, and coincidence, once again surrounded the Victorian, when he and another batsman named Wayne Phillips both scored 132* in Melbourne grade-cricket on the same weekend, during the 1995-96 season.

> ### QUOTE
> *"When I was born my father, certain he had produced an opening bat for Yorkshire and England, set about finding a suitable cricketer's name. His first suggestion was that I be called Herbert Hedley Parkinson in honour of Sutcliffe and Verity, my father's heroes. When this was vetoed by my mother he suggested Michael Melbourne Parkinson in celebration of a recent victory by England in that city. Fortunately my mother, a woman of great commonsense, would have none of it and plain Michael it was. My mother had not realised when she married my father that she was taking on the Yorkshire Cricket Club as well."*
>
> — Michael Parkinson

Brian Lara named his first child Sydney, in celebration of the city where he scored his maiden Test century (277 v Australia in 1992-93): "I chose Sydney because that was where I had my best Test innings. It's a very, very unique name. The other, Taryne, is her mother's choice."

In celebration of Trevor Barsby's century in Queensland's Sheffield Shield final triumph in 1994-95, a Brisbane doctor honoured the batsman when naming his new-born son. Timothy Stuart Barsby Gregg was born on 26 March 1995, the day Barsby scored his match-winning ton. The Queensland captain, Stuart Law, was also honoured in the baby's name.

Appearing for South Australia in the Sheffield Shield-winning XI at the Adelaide Oval in 1995-96 were two Darrens, two Jamies and two Tims. Batting one after the other in the SA line-up was Darren Webber and Darren Lehmann, followed by Jamie Brayshaw and Jamie Siddons and Tim Nielsen and Tim May.

When the touring Australians played Glamorgan at Swansea in 1975, the home-side's batting was opened by Alan Jones and Alan Jones.

Fast bowler Chaminda Vaas, who possesses one of the shortest surnames for a Sri Lankan, certainly makes up for it when you spell out his full name — one that contains 53 letters (Warnakulasooriya Patabendige Ushantha Joseph Chaminda Vaas).

West Indies fast bowler Nixon Alexei McLean was born on the opening day of a top-level US-Soviet summit in 1973, and named by his father after the conference's leaders — American President Richard Nixon and Russia's Alexei Kosygin. His other middle name, McNamara, was chosen in honour of former US Defence Secretary, Robert McNamara. McLean's two younger fast-bowling brothers are Reagan (Ronald Reagan) and Kissinger (former US Secretary of State, Henry Kissinger).

Len Pascoe, the former Australian fast bowler of Yuglosav background, was born with the surname Durtanovich, and appeared under that name as a youngster in a match for the New South Wales Colts in 1969-70.

India's Sachin Tendulkar was named after Sachin Dev Burman, a popular West Bengali folksinger.

Four players by the name of Ijaz Ahmed appeared in first-class cricket matches in Pakistan in the 1989-90 season. Two of them later played Test cricket, and appeared together in the same side in the 1996-97 World Series Cup in Australia.

During the 1980s the Wallsend District Cricket Club in Newcastle had four medium-pace bowlers in its 2nd XI named Craig — Craig Wivell, Craig Hughes, Craig Vickery and Craig Fennings.

A cricket club in Melbourne, the East Malvern juniors, boasted a number of appropriately-named players on its books in 1996-97 — Anthony **Batt**ista, Joshua **Bowling**, Matthew **Field**send and Jeremy **Wick**ett.

Dear Metropolitan,
My name is Batters. One of my top sales consultants is John Boling and another is Tim Baillieu. My secretary's name is Jenny Nunn and that would probably be the score we'd make if we played cricket.
— Letter to *The Age* newspaper, 1997

BIRTHS AND DEATHS

A match of cricket was played on Friday last, near Totteridge, Herts, between two young men of the names of Gregg and Corderoy, which was so well maintained, that forty-three and forty-five runs were made in the first innings. Gregg was caught out after making thirty-two runs in the second innings. Corderoy went in, and made seven runs; he again hit the ball, and ran, but on arriving at the wicket he fell down and expired.

— *The Times*, 1805

During a Test match at Lord's in the early 1980s, a club member died while sitting in the pavilion. So as not to upset those around him, a ground steward was given the gruesome task of sitting next to the corpse to keep him 'company' until the end of the day's play.

Before she passed away in New Zealand in 1996 at the age of 109, Sister Mary Doyle attributed her long life to her love of God and cricket.

A spectator at the West Indies-Pakistan one-day international at Brisbane in 1996-97 was advised, over the public-address system, to report to the match office. His wife had just given birth!

When a West Australian XI took on Zimbabwe in outback Kalgoorlie in 1994-95, the best performers for the Warriors were all born overseas. Mark Lavender, born in Madras, top-scored with 74 while the next highest-scorer was the Zimbabwean-born

Murray Goodwin (52). Brendon Julian, born in New Zealand, was the most successful all-rounder in the match, scoring an unbeaten 22 and taking 3 for 36.

A SELECTION OF AUSTRALIAN FIRST-CLASS CRICKETERS FROM THE 1990s BORN OVERSEAS

Player & State	Birthplace
John Davison (Vic)	Campbell River, Canada
Murray Goodwin (WA)	Harare, Zimbabwe
Steve Herzberg (WA & Tas)	Carshalton, England
Neil Jones (NSW)	Stourport-on-Severn, England
Brendon Julian (WA)	Hamilton, New Zealand
Mark Lavender (WA)	Madras, India
Ken MacLeay (WA)	Bedford-on-Avon, England
Martin McCague (WA)	Larne, Northern Ireland
Phil Marks (NSW)	Harare, Zimbabwe
Neil Maxwell (Vic & NSW)	Lautoka, Fiji
Alan Mullally (WA & Vic)	Southend, England
Tim Nielsen (SA)	London, England
Steve Russell (WA)	Helensville, New Zealand
Chris Smart (Qld)	Port Moresby, PNG
Duncan Spencer (WA)	Nelson, England
Andrew Symonds (Qld)	Birmingham, England
Craig White (Vic)	Morley, England

Fred Smith was a batsman who appeared in three Tests for South Africa, including the country's first — against England in 1888-89. Strangely, no details of either his birth or death exist.

A 14-year-old boy from Perth murdered his four-year-old cousin in 1995, because she'd interrupted him watching cricket on TV. He was sentenced to a seven-year term in a juvenile detention centre.

In 1984 Patrick Miller scored a half-century for his local cricket club in Nottingham, after killing a friend over what to watch on TV. Miller, who was charged with manslaughter, received a four-year gaol term.

In 1951-52 a cricketer was killed in a shooting rampage during a match in the Australian Country Carnival at Adelaide. Arthur Henderson was one of two players shot by a spectator who fired randomly at the players in the game between South-East and Upper North. The man was arrested nearby and charged with murder.

A cricket-playing grandfather committed suicide in 1996 because of his hatred of winter. Sixty year-old Eddie Baxter, who spent most of his time playing cricket in the summer months, suffered from an illness known as 'Seasonal Affective Disorder'. According to his daughter, Baxter even purcashed a satellite dish to watch overseas cricket matches in the hope of making him think it was summer.

In his retirement match, at Cuckfield in Sussex in 1995, Jack Swain, 73, collapsed and died moments after bowling his final over. The match was abandoned, but a farewell in his honour went ahead as scheduled as a mark of respect.

THE COMMENTATORS

Henry Blofeld was hauled before Britain's Broadcasting Standards Council in 1995, for making 'tasteless and racist' remarks during the first England-West Indies Test match at Leeds. 'Blowers' had commented that spectators viewing the game from the balcony of a tall building overlooking the Headingley ground were in the 'Jewish Stand'. Following the Council's ruling that his remarks were unacceptable, the veteran BBC commentator apologised, adding that he very much regretted the lapse.

The late BBC commentator Brian Johnston displayed, for all to see, his total passion for the game — a tattoo on his left arm. It depicted two crossed-cricket bats and a ball.

Former West Indies batsman Gerry Gomez was a busy man during the third Test match against Australia at Georgetown in 1964-65 . . . not only was he a West Indies selector and match-umpire, he was also a radio commentator required to present a daily summary of play.

Before his graduation to the ranks of full-time cricket commentator, the ABC's Alan McGilvray had enjoyed a moderate 20-match first-class cricketing career for New South Wales. Opening the bowling attack on his first-class debut, against Victoria at the MCG in 1933-34, McGilvray took one wicket, but ruined teammate Bill O'Reilly's chances of taking all 10 wickets in an innings. O'Reilly captured 9 for 50, the best return in matches between the two states, while McGilvray took 1 for 51. When it was his time to bat, he strolled out to the middle accompanied by one Don Bradman: "Fancy that, Braddles, isn't it nice how all these people have come out just to see me bat!" McGilvray later recalled that

"Bradman gave me an odd look that I will never forget."

One of the greatest disappointments for McGilvray as a commentator was the day that he, and Keith Miller, flew back to Sydney during the dying moments of the Australia-West Indies Test match at Brisbane in 1960-61. With their commentary duties completed for the day, the pair missed out on being part of cricket history, with the match ending sensationally in a tie.

McGilvray later claimed that, perhaps, the most famous piece of cricket commentary — that of the Brisbane tie — was 'dummied-up': "The ABC naturally enough wanted to keep the tape for archival purposes. And since the one they had wasn't really quite good enough they decided to do another. The team of office staff was taken to the ground armed with typewriters to provide background noise . . . and this time the commentary was spot on, recording the tied Test for all time." The suggestion was hotly disputed by fellow commentator Clive Harburg: "Michael Charlton and I were left to do the commentary after Alan had requested permission to leave the ground before the game was over," adding that McGilvray had "turned his back on history that day and must regret it now."

QUOTE

"For as long as cicadas sing in the Australian heat, so too will cricket on radio be a staple part of the sound of summer."

— Alan McGilvray

THE FIRST-CLASS PLAYING RECORD OF
A.D. McGILVRAY (NSW 1933-34/36-37)

Batting

M	I	NO	Runs	HS	Avge
20	31	3	684	68	24.42

Bowling

R	W	10wm	5wi	BB	Avge
1135	20	-	-	3-35	56.75

Alan Marks, who occasionally calls the cricket for the ABC, lists as his worst moment behind the microphone, a game in Newcastle. Play was held up due to the reflection of the sun off a car windscreen upsetting the batsmen. Marks commented on air about the stupidity of the car's owner for parking in such a position, but then realised, a few minutes later, it was his.

During the first Test against India at Bangalore in 1988-89, almost the entire New Zealand team was struck down with a case of 'Delhi belly'. Five substitutes were used by the Kiwis in the second innings, including commentators and correspondents from Television New Zealand and Radio NZ.

Australian batsman Michael Slater was thrust into the role of TV cricket commentator during the 1996 World Cup, when the rostered crew — including Ian Chappell and Tony Greig — failed to arrive in time.

Chandra Nayudu — the daughter of India's first Test captain C.K. Nayudu — made history in 1976-77, becoming the world's first female cricket commentator when she reported on play during the MCC-Bombay match at Indore.

Max Walker's debut as a commentator on the ABC was one to remember. In his eagerness to get to the microphone, Walker accidentally kneed Alan McGilvray in the back of the head, and sent crashing to the floor all of the scorer's notes and cricket stats: "I was beetroot red with embarrassment, my shirt was saturated in sweat and I hadn't even said a word."

QUOTE
"That bloke could talk under water with a mouthful of marbles."
— Former ABC broadcaster Drew Morphett, on the commentary skills of Max Walker

Brian Johnston amused all during a Test-match commentary when he started chatting about an entirely different 'sporting' event: "Oh, a bit of bad news. Nick in *Neighbours* has strained his ankle falling off his skateboard. He'll be all right, though, ol' Nick. He couldn't go in the race and Matt took his place . . . and I haven't heard whether he won." 'Johnners' was apparently slightly distressed at missing the daily TV soap opera from Australia. When he was away from England, calling the cricket, he made sure someone taped every episode of *Neighbours* — his favourite television show.

Billy Birmingham, who, as 'The Twelfth Man', made a fortune impersonating the Channel 9 commentary team

QUOTE
"I think Richie Benaud would be very happy if I pissed off and Tony Greig is pretty cool about it, but Bill (Lawry) really enjoys it."

— 'The Twelfth Man'

117

A COLLECTION OF CLASSIC ON-AIR CLANGERS

"The Queen's Park Oval. Exactly as its name suggests . . . absolutely round."
— Tony Cozier

"One of the hardest things is to take a caught and bowled off your own bowling."
— Mike Haysman

"He's got Taylor breathing down his throat, or his neck if you like."
— Tony Greig, Channel 9

"Butcher plays this off the black foot."
— Brian Johnston, BBC

"England have won 12. Australia have won 12. So they are pretty even."
— Bill Lawry, Channel 9

"It's a very good witch in Bombay . . . good wicket."
— Greg Ritchie, Channel 9

"Look at Siddons. He's ready to throw like a panther."
— Kim Hughes, Optus Vision

"He's bowled him three wrong-'uns now, and he hasn't picked either of them."
— Bill Lawry, Channel 9

"What a magnificent shot! No, he's out."
— Tony Greig, Channel 9

"That's the second time Maher has been bitten . . . beaten."
— Rod Kilner, ABC Radio

"On the outfield, hundreds of small boys are playing with their balls."
— Rex Alston, BBC

"And the fifth bowler is himself or Harper, or Harper himself."
— Tony Greig, Channel 9

"Border was facing a four-paced prong attack."
— Dave Renneberg, ABC Radio

"Fast bowlers are quick, even at the end of the day. Just watch this — admittedly it's in slow motion."
— Ian Chappell, Channel 9

"For every winner, there has to be a loser in these games."
— Tony Greig, Channel 9

"A very small crowd here today. I can count the people on one hand. Can't be more than 30."
— Michael Abrahamson, SABC

"There were congratulations and high-sixes all round."
— Richie Benaud, Channel 9

"As a result, Tasmania picks up two valuable points, not that they are any value now. The match has already been decided."
— Gerry Collins, ABC Radio

OUR DON BRADMAN

> **QUOTE**
>
> *"Don Bradman is bigger than Babe."*
>
> — Bowral Mayor Jim Tuddenham, in 1996, on the area's two major tourist attractions: The Don and film-making

Don Bradman's first hundred came at the age of 12. It was scored in his first organised match — an imposing 115* for Bowral High School (156) against Mittagong School.

It was around this time that the young Don caught the attention of the press, with the first known newspaper article about him appearing in *Smith's Weekly* (c1920): *Saw a curious thing at a junior cricket match at Bowral (NSW) recently. Don Bradman (crack bat) sent a ball over the boundary fence. It struck half a brick, rebounded on to a fence post, poised there for an appreciable time and ran along the top of the palings the whole length of a panel of fencing before descending outside the boundary.*

The first first-class cricket match that Don Bradman saw was the fifth Test against England at the Sydney Cricket Ground in 1920-21. The next one he attended, he played in — New South Wales against South Australia in Adelaide in 1927-28.

The bat with which Bradman scored 212 against England in 1936-37 sold for a record £26,844 at auction in London in 1996. With a reserve price of some £500-700, the price paid shattered the previous highest successful bid for a historic bat — an amount of £1300, in 1981, for one used by Jack Hobbs.

In 1979 Bradman was made a Companion of the Order of Australia — the highest decoration under the nation's honours

> **QUOTE**
>
> *"About the last thing I ever wanted in life was a knighthood, and even today some forty years after the event, I find it difficult to come to terms with a life where old and valued friends insist on calling me Sir, instead of Don, simply because they think it is protocol. But I have consciously shouldered these burdens because I felt that I was the medium through which cricket could achieve a higher status and gain maximum support from the people, not only in Australia but throughout the world."*

system. In 1949 he had become only the second Test cricketer after England's 'Plum' Warner to be knighted.

In his 80 Test-match innings for Australia, Bradman was never stumped and was run out just once, for 58 against England at Adelaide in 1928-29 — his first season of Test cricket. He was caught 34 times and bowled on 24 occasions, while he was out hit wicket only once in his entire first-class career, against India at Brisbane in 1947-48.

HOW BRADMAN WAS DISMISSED IN TEST CRICKET

Caught	34
Bowled	24
LBW	6
Caught and bowled	4
Hit wicket	1
Run out	1
Stumped	-
Not out	10
Total Innings	**80**

QUOTE

"Selectorship — a fascinating job really, despite its complexities."

— Don Bradman

"Sir Donald was easily the best selector I came across anywhere in the world."

— Richie Benaud

In 1971 Bradman stepped down as an Australian Test selector, a position he had held with distinction since 1936. During his time on the committee, in which 151 Tests were played, Australia lost, on average, just one match in five.

The *New York Times*, a newspaper that rarely acknowledges cricket, once described Bradman as the game's 'unchallenged shining light', 'the wild man of the wicket' and 'the ring-tailed wallaby of the cricket crease'.

In 1996 the Royal Australian Mint recognised the unique qualities of Don Bradman by releasing a special five dollar coin. A few months prior to its official release, the Mint broke with tradition by allowing a sneak preview of the coin, with one used for the toss at the Prime Minister's XI-West Indies one-day cricket match at Canberra's Manuka Oval.

The following year, Australia's postal service paid Bradman the ultimate accolade by issuing two 45c stamps in his honour. The stamps were the first in the so-called 'Australian Legends' series, to be released annually, with Bradman becoming the first living person, other than The Queen, to have his portrait featured on a stamp released by Australia Post.

In another world first, a special version of the stamps in twenty-four carat gold was made, with one set presented to Sir Donald; another to the Parliament of Australia.

The Don Bradman $5 coin issued in 1996 and one of the Don Bradman 45c stamps released in 1997

The national post office box number for the Australian Broadcasting Corporation is 9994 — Don Bradman's Test-career batting average (99.94).

Returning home from a round of golf in 1996, Bradman was booked for speeding. He was clocked doing 72 kilometres per hour in a 60-zone, on Adelaide's former Grand Prix racing circuit, and fined $173. Not long after his speeding offence became publicly known, the traffic policeman who nabbed Sir Donald was interviewed on Channel 9's *A Current Affair*.

123

Mr Don Bradman, the famous cricketer, was present at the Grand Opera House last night to hear his song *'Everyday is a Rainbow Day for Me'* which is introduced in the pantomime *Beauty and The Beast*. The song, composed by Mr Bradman to words by Mr Jack Lumsdaine, was sung by Miss Elsie Hosking, and proved pleasantly melodious and sentimental, with a refrain in which saxophones and brasses vigorously supported the vocal theme.

After the song there was great applause for the composer as he walked on the stage. Mr Bradman said he had enjoyed very much the experience of his composition sung in public.

— Newspaper report (1930s)

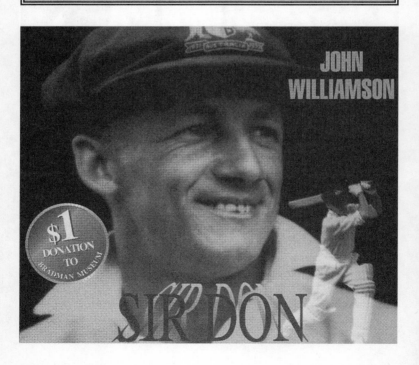

Don Bradman was the first cricketer in the world to be the subject of a recorded song. The 1930 78 rpm record *'Our Don Bradman'*, written by Jack O'Hagan and sung by Australian baritone Art Leonard, was so popular that it sold out within a matter of days.

'OUR DON BRADMAN'

Who is it that all Australia raves about?
Who has won our very highest praise?
Now is it Amy Johnson, or little Mickey Mouse?
No! it's just a country lad who's bringing down the house
And he's our Don Bradman
And I ask you is he any good?
Our Don Bradman
As a batsman he can sure lay on the wood
For when he goes in to bat
He knocks every record flat
For there isn't anything he cannot do
Our Don Bradman, every Aussie dips his lid to you
Our Don Bradman, now I ask you is he any good?
Our Don Bradman, as a batsman he is certainly 'Plum Pud'!
Tate and Larwood meet their fate
For it's always shut the gate, when the boy from Bowral hits four after four
Our Don Bradman, what a welcome waits for you back home.

— Jack O'Hagan (1930)

The *Sydney Morning Herald*'s ever-popular 'Column 8' was first published on 11 January 1947 and remains the longest-running column in Australian newspaper history. Its first-ever item was about The Don: *VALUES. Don Bradman, Test cricketer, can't remember the number of autographs he's signed — "must run into many thousands." Marcus Oliphant, atom expert, can. He's never been asked for one.*

> ## QUOTE
> *"I was popped in a metaphorical glass cage to be peered at or discussed. I am no longer prepared to accept being seriously introduced as simply some-one's son. I am an individual not a social souvenir."*
> — Sir Don's son, John Bradman, who changed his surname by deed-poll to Bradsen in 1972

"I don't know why they make such a fuss about Don. After all, he was just a cricketer." — a comment attributed to Don Bradman's sister, May Glover, who lived in Bowral until her death in 1996.

A horse named Bradman finished third in her first race at the Caufield track in Melbourne in 1997. The Bart Cummings-trained horse came from the same stable as Sir Donald, which came first in a maiden event in 1996.

Bradman once had a flower named after him. The 'Don Bradman Dahlia' was so-named because of 'its strength and vigorous growth. In colour it is toned from a deep orange to chrome-yellow with a blush of pink'.

Former Prime Minister Sir Robert Menzies, a good friend of Bradman, once privately floated the idea of The Don becoming Australian High Commissioner to London.

The average time Bradman needed to reach 50 in first-class cricket was 67 minutes. For 100 it was 144 minutes and 255 minutes for 200. The average length of each of Bradman's completed innings in the first-class game was two hours and 14 minutes.

A major television special, presented by Ray Martin, on the life and times of Bradman — *Don Bradman: 87 Not Out*, aired on Channel 9 in 1996 with an audience of 600,000 in Sydney. Nationally, the program was watched by 1,600,000 across the five major capital cities.

Bradman, who rarely grants media interviews, agreed to take part provided funds raised through its televising went to the Bradman Museum in Bowral. Within 40 hours of the TV special going to air, $780,000 was collected, with the Federal Government contributing $100,000.

'Rampaging' Roy Slaven: "I'm not knocking Ray at all. I think Ray did a magnificent job. It was a very engaging interview, but for me it was a wasted opportunity. There are so many things I want to know about Don Bradman. I want to know about his cardio-vascular system. I wanna know about his reflexology. I want to know how the old bloke would still cope. Put him in the nets with Courtney Walsh or Curtly Ambrose comin' down at him. And in another net, with just a normal 87-year-old standing there, and compare the two. I just wanna see what his reflexes are like. I want to see his DNA. I want to see it held up. I want to see the bloke cut open. Let's really get in and have a look what is ... what made Don, the great Don that he still could be. I'd like to see him coming back. I want to see him with the baggy, and the gear and the old stupid-looking bat. I just saw it as a wasted opportunity."

H.G. Nelson: "You know, Roy, I've always wanted to see The Don nude. I think that was the missed opportunity for mine. There was a chance to show the people of Australia, what the people of South Australia have enjoyed for years now, and that is a normal 87-year-old strolling about David Jones, Rundle Mall, catching the Bay tram ... totally buffed."

— From ABC TV's *Club Buggery*

Bradman is the only Australian batsman to have scored 1000 Test runs in a calendar year in fewer than ten matches. In 1948, his final year of Test cricket, Bradman scored 1025 runs in just eight matches, with a top score of 201 against India in Sydney.

At the SCG in 1933-34, Bradman marked his last appearance for New South Wales by scoring a century (128), one that included

21 boundaries. For the first time in his first-class career, Bradman hit a six — with four in all. Three came during a single over, bowled by Victoria's 'Chuck' Fleetwood-Smith.

Richard Cashman, an associate professor at the University of NSW, once conducted a statistical survey into the drawing power of individual players at cricket matches. He concluded that on days when Bradman batted, average crowds were a phenomenal 91 per cent higher.

> **QUOTE**
>
> *"People who had never been to a cricket match before, who did not know a bat from a ball, flocked to see Bradman. It was usual to see thousands leave the ground when Bradman was dismissed. The atmosphere and most of the interest in the game walked back to the pavilion."*
>
> — Jack Fingleton

Five times during his Test career, Bradman scored more than half of Australia's innings on his own. On three occasions, his dominance contributed to an Australian win; the other two matches, in which he scored triple-centuries, were drawn.

His Score	Team's Score	%	Match	Venue	Season	Result
334	566	59.01	3rd Test v England	Leeds	1930	D
299*	513	58.28	4th Test v South Africa	Adelaide	1931-32	W
103*	191	53.93	2nd Test v England	Melbourne	1932-33	W
304	584	52.05	4th Test v England	Leeds	1934	D
226	450	50.22	1st Test v South Africa	Brisbane	1931-32	W

Australian actor Gary Sweet, who played the part of Don Bradman in the TV mini-series *Bodyline*, appeared in a celebrity cricket match at the SCG in 1994-95. Appearing for the World XI against the Bradman XI, Sweet marked his appearance by claiming a wicket with his first delivery.

In 1995 12-year-old Tristan Tatt, a member of the under-14 A-grade South Morang cricket team in Melbourne, appeared in a 'Test match' for Australia. Tristan was chosen from a field of 30 hopefuls who auditioned for the part of Don Bradman in a Weet-Bix television commercial.

Of the sixteen ducks Bradman made in first-class cricket, six were 'first-ball', while another three were 'second-ball'.

A BREAKDOWN OF BRADMAN'S INDIVIDUAL FIRST-CLASS SCORES

Score	Innings	Runs
0	16	0
1-49	136	2820
50-99	69	4897
100-199	80	10,906
200-299	31	7288
300-399	5	1704
400 +	1	452
Total	**338**	**28,067**

Charles Davis, an Australian sports statistician, claims that so exceptional is Bradman, it would take over 100,000 years, and 1,000,000 players, for another cricketer of his standard to emerge.

EXTRAS

In 1989 viewers of the Yorkshire Television network were invited to ring up and record their opinions on Yorkshire cricket. When callers got through, they were greeted with a rather unusual recorded message: "Hello, this is Barbara. I hope I can help you by talking about something that men worry about." And it wasn't the state of cricket in Yorkshire. The phone service, detailing improvements for sexual performance, prompted an influx of complaints, with Telecom accepting blame, citing a computer fault.

A vasectomy operation was donated by some local doctors to a Gloucestershire cricket club in 1995 for a fund-raising auction. It went for £90.

A club match in England in 1988 ended in humiliating defeat for Hatfield Town, after losing their last five wickets in the final over. Chasing Barnly Dun's 9 for 166, the Hatfield XI committed cricket's version of hari-kari recording five consecutive run-outs and handing a most-unexpected victory to their opposition.

Funny things happen in New Zealand . . . no more bizarre, an incident in 1996-97 when Wellington cricket officials employed a male stripper to streak at a one-day match at the Basin Reserve. The streaker did his dash, waved to the crowd and was subsequently arrested by a female police officer, who turned out to be another professional entertainer, paid for by the cricket association. The local police force was unimpressed, with the district commander Gerry Cuneen describing the incident as one of no entertainment value: "We do not condone that sort of conduct. It was trespass on the grounds which amounts to offensive behaviour."

The long-running comic strip *Fred Bassett* raised a few concerned eyebrows in 1996 when it attempted to portray a village cricket match. The strip had the dog's owner making his first appearance for the local cricket team — using a baseball bat. It's thought that the cartoon may have been altered for the American market.

Major Ron Ferguson, the father of the Duchess of York, and recognised polo fanatic, opened an indoor cricket school in Hampshire in 1996. According to England's *Daily Telegraph* "his answer to recent personal catastrophes has been to immerse himself in the rolling arable fields of Dummer Down Farm, and to switch from the dashing world of polo to the safer, less contrived boundaries of the cricket field, where the people are 'much more worthwhile'."

Just one of the many embarrassments to hit the Royal Family in recent times . . . Prince Charles was bowled first-ball by a 10-year-old at a junior cricket display at The Oval in 1995.

Buckingham Palace issued a rare public apology in 1996, after Prince Philip had compared cricket bats to guns in the debate over a ban on such weapons in the wake of a massacre at a school in Scotland earlier in the year. The Duke, a keen game shooter and cricket follower, had stated "if a cricketer, for instance, suddenly decided to go into a school and batter a lot of people to death with a cricket bat, which he could do very easily, I mean are you going to ban cricket bats?"

> Judging by the success of the Royal Boxing Day Pheasant Shoot, and after Prince Philip's statement that guns are no more dangerous than cricket bats, perhaps the Duke should be coaching the English cricket team.
>
> — Letter to the Editor, *The Australian*
>
> It has been reported that royal game reserves in Britain are now resounding to the sounds of willow on pheasant, accompanied by joyous cries of "Owzat, M'Lord?"
>
> — Letter to the Editor, *Sydney Morning Herald*

A leading Pakistan fortune teller predicted in 1997 that Imran Khan would be murdered, and that his wife, Jemima, would suffer a miscarriage. Writing in the Lahore newspaper *Frontier Post*, Fawad Wasim also predicted that Imran's political aspirations may come to fruition . . ."However, the Jewish lobby will be behind Imran's death, and Jemima will be a part of this conspiracy."

In his first Test series for South Africa, against England in 1938-39, opening batsman Pieter van der Bijl was dismissed in a different way in his first five innings — lbw and bowled, at Johannesburg, caught and hit wicket at Cape Town and run out at Durban. Hugh Tayfield experienced a similar pattern in his first five Test innings, against Australia in 1949-50 — lbw and caught at Johannesburg, stumped and bowled at Cape Town and run out at Durban.

Australian historian Manning Clark was an enthusiastic wicket-keeper/batsman who played district cricket in Melbourne and appeared in three first-class matches for Oxford University in 1939. From six innings he made 87 runs, a top score of 22, and a first-class average of 14.50. His best score with the bat was at Melbourne Grammar School, with an unbeaten knock of 165 against Geelong College.

British writer A. A. Milne, and his son, Christopher Robin Milne — the star of the best-selling book *When We Were Very Young* — both played cricket at school. A. A. Milne played for two seasons at Westminster, while Christopher was captain at Stowe School.

LETTER TO THE EDITOR —
THE TIMES, 23 AUGUST 1928

Sir, I must make my contribution to cricket history; the only one I am likely to make. In 1899 I was playing for Westminster v Charterhouse, the match of the year. Somehow or other the batsman at the other end managed to get out before I did, and the next man came in, all a-tremble with nervousness. He hit his first ball straight up in the air, and called wildly for a run. We all ran — he, I and the bowler. My partner got underneath the ball first, and in a spasm of excitement jumped up and hit it again as hard as he could. There was no appeal. He burst into tears, so to speak, and hurried back to the pavilion. Whether he would have run away to sea the next day, or gone to Africa and shot big game, we shall never know, for luckily he restored his self-respect a few hours later by bowling Charterhouse out and winning the match for us. But here, for your Cricket Correspondent, is a genuine case of 'Out, obstructing the field'.

— A.A. Milne

QUOTE

"Hey, Greigy. This champagne's all right, but the blackcurrant jam tastes of fish."

— Derek Randall, to Tony Greig, on eating caviar

A barman who worked at Lord's was sentenced to three months gaol in 1992, charged with punching and kicking a spectator who had dared to change his drinks order.

Play was halted for gastronomic reasons in a Castle Cup match in South Africa in 1994-95, after Border's Daryll Cullinan hit a six that landed in a frying pan cooking calamari. It took ten minutes for the ball to cool down and for the grease to be removed. Even then, the bowler — Boland's Roger Telemachus — was unable to grip the ball properly and it had to be replaced.

A survey undertaken in 1994 revealed that of all the ICC Associate Members, Bangladesh had the most cricket clubs (1588) and players (93,000). Next on the list was Canada, with 502 clubs and 23,904 players.

In 1987 an Indian man posing as Test cricketer Chetan Sharma signed up as a player for the English cricket club Wakefield. The imposter failed to turn up for the first match of the season and Wakefield played with ten men. After realising they'd been conned, Wakefield then employed West Indian fast bowler George Ferris. Unfortunately he, too, failed to make it to his first match, and again Wakefield played with only ten on the field.

English club cricketer Wayne Ratcliffe received a five-year playing ban in 1995 for urinating on the pitch during a match for Newmillerdam: "By the time a wicket fell I was desperate. I turned towards some trees and answered the call of nature. Hardly anyone saw!"

Paul Crabb, a village cricketer in England, was sent running nearly half a kilometre to field a ball during a match in North Devon in 1996. After sailing over the boundary, the ball bounced over a hedge and rolled down a hill towards the town of Hele. Upon retrieving the ball, Crabb decided he'd had enough exercise for one day and rather than walk up the hill, he caught a bus back to the ground.

ALLAN FELS' 'DREAM TEAM'

Jack Hobbs
Bill Ponsford
Don Bradman (c)
Graeme Pollock
Viv Richards
Garry Sobers
Keith Miller
Alan Knott
Sydney Barnes
Dennis Lillee
Bill O'Reilly

Allan Fels, appointed chairman of the Australian Competition and Consumer Commission in 1991, is an avid cricket fan, who, as a child, was lucky enough to have a former WA bowler — Charlie Puckett — as his personal coach.

In 1950 a young Fels, bowling wrist leg-spin, took all 10 wickets for his Perth school, St Louis, against Scotch College. He later went on to play in the Perth grade competition and for the University of Western Australia.

India's R. Patel recorded one of the game's most inauspicious Test debuts, when he opened the bowling in both innings against New Zealand at Bombay in 1988-89 without taking a wicket. He also made a pair of ducks in his only Test-match appearance, out both times to the bowling of Richard Hadlee.

A life-size photograph of Merv Hughes was an official exhibit during proceedings in the 1996 'backpacker' murder case. The picture of the former Australian fast bowler, and one of Ivan Milat, the

---

QUOTE
"I watch cricket, and my idea of a Merv Hughes moustache is that it sweeps back a bit."

— Ivan Milat

---

man convicted of killing seven backpackers, was shown to the New South Wales Supreme Court jury so their moustaches could be compared. A British tourist who was allegedly kidnapped by Milat, claimed in court that his attacker had a 'Merv Hughes-style' moustache. In his final address to the jury, the Crown Prosecutor Mark Tedeschi said it was "a very accurate and very colourful description."

While playing in a club match in England in 1989, Linden Park's John Holden was shot by an airgun pellet fielding near the boundary.

A highly unusual incident befell Vince Bruno in a D-grade cricket match in Victoria in 1994-95, when he was dismissed twice in a hat-trick. Playing against Fairfield in the Jika Cricket Association competition, Bruno and his partner were dismissed in successive balls by W. Dunmore, with Thomastown all out for 118. Following on, the two batsmen were directed to open the second innings. Dunmore took Bruno's wicket with his first ball, and thus gained one of cricket's most bizarre hat-tricks.

A village match between Curdridge and Medstead near Southampton in 1982 was brought to an abrupt halt when a hot-air balloon ran out of fuel and landed on the pitch.

Hayden Cordingley was recorded in the scorebook for the Cliffe-Yalding match in Kent in 1996 as 'absent, baby-sitting, 0'.

The Korweinguboora cricket team in Victoria progressed through the 1963-64 season undefeated. Playing in the Daylesford and District Cricket Association, what made this team so extraordinary was that all 11 members were left-handed.

Richard Digance, a popular London folk singer, wrote a cricket novel, *Run Out in the Country*, that was published in 1983. The author boasts another cricketing claim to fame — he was born on the same day, and in the same hospital, as the England left-arm bowler John Lever.

For the final Test of the 1989-90 Test series against England, at St John's, the West Indies brought back Eldine Baptiste for his first match since 1984. Baptiste ended his ten-match career for the Windies without ever tasting defeat.

When India's Mohammad Azharuddin appeared in the first Test against South Africa at Ahmedabad in 1996-97, he became the first cricketer in history to play against all the other eight Test nations, at home and abroad.

The biggest crowd for a day's Test cricket remains the 90,800 that turned up for the second day of the fifth Test against the West Indies at Melbourne in 1960-61. When it comes to small crowds, the first Test between Zimbabwe and New Zealand at Bulawayo in 1992-93 must take the cake. It's been said that when play began on the first morning, the only ones who turned up were the players and umpires, two players' wives, five journalists, two security guards and two officials. No spectators were to be seen.

Zimbabwean cricketer Craig Evans recorded an unusual double with the bat in a first-class match between Mashonaland and the visiting Northamptonshire county side in 1994-95. In the first innings he was forced to retire with his score on four to attend a court hearing for a traffic offence. He later resumed his innings, finishing with an unbeaten six. In the second innings, he scored a century (102), contributing to his side's six-wicket victory.

Sri Lanka's Arjuna Ranatunga, who played in his country's inaugural Test as a schoolboy, first came to prominence in an under-15 match for Ananda College in 1977-78. Captaining the side, Ranatunga scored 315*, with 48 fours and 12 sixes, and took 11 wickets for 24.

After turning 50, John King — who played in a Test for England against Australia at Lord's in 1909 — was still good enough to take 100 wickets and score over 5000 runs in first-class cricket. In 1923 King, aged 52, scored a double-century (205) for Leicestershire against Hampshire — a unique achievement in

England's County Championship.

Another 52-year-old, George Cox Snr took 17 for 206 for Sussex against Warwickshire in 1926. He, too, passed the 1000 run-100 wicket double after the age of 50. During the same season, a 54-year-old Willie Quaife scored 1000 runs and took 78 wickets in first-class matches for Warwickshire — the best all-round performance by a player over the age of 50.

PLAYERS AGED OVER 50 WHO SCORED 1000 RUNS AND TOOK 100 WICKETS IN ENGLAND'S COUNTY CHAMPIONSHIP

	M	Runs	Wkts
Willie Quaife (Warwickshire)	161	6237	303
John King (Leicestershire)	112	5184	100
George Cox Snr (Sussex)	90	1810	199
Wilfred Rhodes (Yorkshire)	71	1422	230
Ernest Robson (Somerset)	57	1134	155

A Danish cricketer by the name of Lars Hansen had a decent match in 1968, when he scored 236* and, with the ball, captured 5 for 20 and 8 for 16, including the hat-trick. His remarkable all-round double came in a junior match for the Svanholm club against Ringsted.

A cricket match at The Oval in 1796 saw a team of one-legged pensioners pitted against a one-armed XI.

South African batsman Daryll Cullinan, whose highest first-class score is 337, found himself in Room No. 337 at his hotel in Rawalpindi during the 1996 World Cup.

Max Immelmann, the famous German airman who presided over his country's fighter tactics during World War I, was shot down and killed in action by a future first-class cricketer. In 1922-23 George McCubbin scored 97 for Transvaal, batting at No.10, against Rhodesia at Bulawayo, adding a record 221 runs for the ninth wicket with Neville Lindsay (160*).

'IT'S ALL HAPPENING'

Cricket enthusiasts are notably obsessed by statistics but there's a figure they don't ever mention. In a six-hour day of Test cricket there is only about half an hour of actual play.

The figure is easily calculated. Time how long it takes from the moment the ball goes dead to the moment the bowler starts a run-up. On a conservative average, it's 30 seconds for a quick bowler and 15 seconds for a spinner. Suppose (generously) that quicks and spinners share the bowling equally — that's an average of 22.5 seconds between balls or a total of three hours 22 minutes in which, by definition, nothing is happening.

Add to that the time taken between overs, about 45 seconds each time (total 1 hour 7 minutes); between the fall of a wicket and the next ball faced, about 220 seconds each time for, say, eight wickets (total 29 minutes); and at drinks, 220 seconds (total 7 minutes) and you get a total of something like five hours 34 minutes in which nothing much is happening other the ball being relayed back to the bowler, fieldsmen being moved and so on. No wonder they invented one-day cricket!

— Letter to the Editor, *Sydney Morning Herald* (1996)

T. Brown, who was batting in New Zealand's Pickard Shield at Pahiatua in 1973-74, will long remember his dismissal at the hands of R. Lambeth from Central Hawkes Bay. Brown whacked one ball with tremendous force towards Lambeth fielding at backward short-leg, who ducked, rather than be hit. Quickly regaining his ground, he spun around in search of the ball, but to no avail. Lambeth eventually found it — in his pocket — and Bush was given out.

A similar, quite extraordinary, incident involved Richard Fry, an opening batsman with the Manly club in Sydney. In a match against Wests in 1996-97, Fry, on 46, despatched the ball towards the boundary, a shot that would have brought up his half-century. Marc Seymour, fielding at silly mid-on, tried to get out of the way, but the ball hit him on the foot and ran up his trouser-leg. That's where the ball stayed, and after some deliberation, the umpires declared that Fry was out.

In 1894 Yorkshire won 12 of its 15 matches in the County Championship — an 80 per cent success rate — yet was unable to win the title. In 1955 they won 75 per cent of their matches, 21 out of 28, and again failed to take the trophy.

Playing for St Patrick's College against St Bernard's at Wellington in 1973-74, 13-year-old Stephen Lane held on to a world-record 14 catches. Fielding at forward short-leg, the schoolboy took seven catches in each innings.

During a television news report of the New Zealand-Sri Lanka Test match at Wellington in 1982-83, TVNZ showed footage of selector Frank Cameron fast asleep, only awakening at the fall of a wicket. Cameron complained to the network that he'd been sleeping at the lunch break, and not during play as indicated by their report. TVNZ was forced to apologise for its misleading editing.

The first first-class match in New Zealand to result in a tie was in 1873-74 — Wellington made 63 and 118, while Nelson scored, appropriately, 111, and 70.

Australia's Jack Blackham appeared in 35 Tests, all of which were against England. England's Archie MacLaren also made 35 Test appearances, all against Australia.

During the 1996 World Cup an Islamabad cardiologist issued a warning for heart patients to avoid watching the India-Pakistan quarter-final match. While admitting the sport was definitely healthy, Nasir Moin claimed that watching the game on television could have fatal consequences for some viewers: "The anxiety gets the better of human arteries."

On the eve of the 1996-97 Australia-West Indies Test series, the Salvation Army's newspaper *The War Cry* carried a front-page article on Shane Warne. While accepting the faith that the Australian team may place in the extraordinary match-winning ability of Warne, it questioned the term 'saviour' used by a journalist in an article in a national newspaper: "*The War Cry* respects Warne's prodigious bowling skills, but suggests the term 'saviour' is best reserved for the one who earned it suffering on a cross for the sins of humanity. No matter how capable a cricketer is, he or she is dependent on time, chance and the twists and turns of sports. God, on the other hand, did not leave things to chance."

Sri Lankan batsman Sanath Jayasuriya was one of the judges at the 1996 Miss World competition in Bangalore.

The inaugural Test between England and Zimbabwe — at Bulawayo in 1996-97 — was the first match in Test history to end

---

QUOTE

"We murdered them and they know it. We flippin' hammered them. We steamrollered all over them."

— England coach David Lloyd, after the drawn first Test match against Zimbabwe at Bulawayo in 1996-97

"This 'we murdered you and you know it' business is frankly monotonous. I'm sorry to say but we don't know it. They're clutching at thin air as far as I'm concerned, and conning themselves into thinking they've played well."

— Zimbabwean captain Alistair Campbell

in a draw with the scores level (Zimbabwe 376 & 234, England 406 & 6-204). The second Test at Harare was also drawn; the series a stalemate at 0-0.

England and Zimbabwe were the poorest performers at Test level during the calendar year of '96 — the African nation were the wooden-spooners with no victories in eight Tests, while England came second-last, commanding an eleven per cent success rate, with one win in nine.

QUOTE

Allan Lamb: *"I condone anyone who tampers with the ball."*

Charles Gray, QC: *"Um yes, I think you mean condemn, don't you?"*

Lamb: *"Yes sir. Condemn."*

— From the Ian Botham v Imran Khan 'ball-tampering' court case, 1996

References

Books:

Who's Who of Cricketers—Philip Bailey, Philip Thorn and Peter Wynne-Thomas (Guild Publishing, 1984)

Cricket: A History of its Growth and Development Throughout the World — Rowland Bowen (Eyre & Spottiswoode, 1970)

Test Cricket Lists — Graham Dawson and Charlie Wat (Five Mile Press, 1996)

Cricket's Far Horizons — Ian Ferguson (Rex Thompson & Family Pty Ltd, 1996)

The Wisden Book of Test Cricket — Bill Frindall (Macdonald Queen Anne Press, 1985)

Hat-Tricks — Kersi Meher-Homji (Kangaroo Press, 1995)

Allan's Australian Cricket Annual — Allan Miller (Allan Miller, various years)

Bat and Pad: Writings on Australian Cricket 1804-1984 — Pat Mullins and Philip Derriman (Oxford University Press, 1984)

The Oxford Companion to Australian Cricket (Oxford University Press, 1996)

Wisden Cricketers' Almanack (John Wisden & Co Ltd, various years)

Magazines:

Australian Cricket, The Cricketer, Inside Edge, Wisden Cricket Monthly

Newspapers:

The Australian, The Canberra Times, Daily Telegraph, Herald Sun, Sydney Morning Herald

Picture Credits:

Auspic, Australia Post, Australian Broadcasting Corporation, Colman's, *Daily Mirror*, EMI Records, John L. Hansen Organisation, *Herald Sun*, John Laws, New Caledonia Post & Telecommunications Office, Office of the Prime Minister, Royal Australian Mint, Sunset Souvenir Post Cards. Every effort has been made to trace copyright owners. However, if there have been any omissions apologies are extended, and any acknowledgments will be made in any subsequent edition.